C# PROGRAMMING FOR BEGINNERS

A Step-by-Step Guide to Learning C# and Building Windows Applications

THOMPSON CARTER

TABLE OF CONTENTS

Introduction

Welcome to *Mastering C# Programming: A Complete Guide to Windows Forms Development*. Whether you're new to programming or already have some experience with other languages, this book will guide you through the essential concepts and techniques required to master C# and build robust Windows Forms applications. Over the next few chapters, you'll learn not only the syntax and structure of C#, but also how to create fully functional, interactive desktop applications for Windows.

Why C# and Windows Forms?

C# is a modern, versatile, and powerful programming language developed by Microsoft. It is widely used in a range of applications, from web and desktop development to mobile and cloud computing. Its simplicity and ease of use, combined with a powerful set of libraries and tools, make C# one of the most popular programming languages today.

Windows Forms, or **WinForms**, is one of the oldest and most widely-used frameworks for building desktop applications in C#. It provides a set of controls and components that you can use to create graphical user interfaces (GUIs) for your applications. Despite the rise of newer frameworks like WPF (Windows Presentation Foundation) and UWP (Universal Windows Platform), Windows

Forms remains a favorite for many developers due to its simplicity and ease of use.

This book is designed to give you a comprehensive understanding of both C# and Windows Forms, enabling you to create visually rich, user-friendly applications. Whether you're looking to build a small utility app, a business solution, or something more complex, this book provides the foundational knowledge you need.

What You'll Learn in This Book

- **C# Fundamentals**: We'll begin with the core concepts of C# programming, such as variables, data types, control flow (if-else, loops), methods, and classes. You'll learn how to write clean, efficient code and explore key principles like object-oriented programming (OOP), which is essential for building scalable and maintainable applications.

- **Windows Forms Development**: Once you've mastered the basics of C#, we'll dive into the world of Windows Forms. You'll learn how to create user interfaces with buttons, labels, text boxes, and other controls. We'll cover event handling, data binding, and how to create interactive applications that respond to user input.

- **Advanced Topics**: As you progress, you'll explore more advanced features such as working with databases using ADO.NET, integrating external libraries and APIs, multithreading, and creating custom controls. We'll also cover important best practices to help you write clean, maintainable, and efficient code.

- **Practical Examples and Projects**: Throughout the book, we'll guide you through real-world examples and projects, such as building a simple progress bar, fetching data from a public API, and packaging your application for deployment. These hands-on projects will help solidify your understanding and give you practical experience building applications with C# and Windows Forms.

- **Debugging and Testing**: Debugging is an essential skill for every developer. We'll teach you how to use Visual Studio's debugging tools effectively, including breakpoints, step-through debugging, and inspecting variables. We'll also cover unit testing, ensuring that your code is reliable and bug-free.

Who This Book is For

This book is ideal for:

- **Beginner developers** who are new to C# and Windows Forms.

- **Intermediate developers** who want to deepen their knowledge of C# and explore Windows Forms in more detail.

- **Experienced developers** looking to refresh their skills, adopt best practices, and learn advanced C# techniques.

You don't need to have prior experience with C# or Windows Forms to get started. Each chapter builds on the previous one, so you can follow along even if you're just beginning your programming journey.

How to Use This Book

This book is structured to be a comprehensive guide for both learning and reference. Each chapter introduces key concepts and then provides hands-on examples that demonstrate how to apply those concepts in a practical, real-world context. You'll also find summaries, key takeaways, and exercises at the end of each chapter to help reinforce what you've learned.

- **Step-by-step examples**: Each concept is explained in detail, and examples are provided to help you see how it works in practice.
- **Hands-on projects**: The book includes practical projects that give you experience creating fully functional Windows Forms applications.
- **Best practices and tips**: Along the way, we'll discuss best practices that will help you write clean, maintainable, and efficient code.

By the end of this book, you will have a solid foundation in C# and Windows Forms development. You will be equipped to create your own Windows desktop applications, integrate external libraries and

APIs, debug your code effectively, and follow best practices for clean and maintainable software development.

Conclusion

Programming is a skill that grows with consistent practice and application. By the time you finish this book, you will have learned both the fundamentals and advanced techniques in C# and Windows Forms. You'll be able to build full-featured applications with user-friendly interfaces and take your programming skills to the next level.

So, let's get started with mastering C# and Windows Forms development. Turn the page and begin your journey to becoming a skilled C# developer!

Chapter 1: Introduction to C# Programming

Topics:

1. **Overview of C#** C# (pronounced "C-sharp") is a modern, object-oriented programming language developed by Microsoft as part of the .NET ecosystem. It is designed to be simple, powerful, and type-safe. C# is used to build a wide variety of applications, from desktop applications to web services and mobile apps. It has become one of the most widely used programming languages, especially for Windows application development, game development (with Unity), and enterprise-level software.

   Why C#?

   - C# is **type-safe**, meaning that it checks for type errors during compilation, which helps reduce runtime errors.
   - It is a **modern language**, designed with simplicity and productivity in mind. Its syntax is clear and easy to learn, making it an excellent choice for beginners.
   - C# is **multi-paradigm**, meaning you can write both object-oriented code and functional code in it.

o The language benefits from a **rich set of libraries** and **strong tooling support**, including the popular IDE, Visual Studio.

2. **History of C#** C# was introduced in the year 2000 by Microsoft as part of its .NET initiative. It was developed under the leadership of Anders Hejlsberg, a Danish software engineer known for his work on Turbo Pascal and Delphi. C# was created to be a language that could leverage the power of the .NET Framework, offering features like garbage collection, exception handling, and a rich class library.

C# initially drew influences from languages such as C, C++, and Java but was designed to be simpler and safer. Over time, C# has grown and evolved, introducing new features like LINQ (Language Integrated Query), async/await for asynchronous programming, and the ability to work with multiple programming paradigms.

The language is constantly updated with new features and improvements, ensuring that it remains a strong choice for modern software development.

3. **Why C# is a Great Language for Beginners**

o **Simple syntax**: The syntax of C# is similar to other popular languages, such as Java and C++. This makes it easier for beginners to transition to more advanced programming concepts.

o **Rich library support**: C# comes with extensive built-in libraries in the .NET framework, which helps simplify many common programming tasks, such as file handling, data access, and networking.

o **Object-Oriented Programming (OOP)**: C# is object-oriented, meaning it organizes code around objects and classes. This helps developers write clean, reusable code, which is easier to maintain and scale.

o **Good documentation and support**: C# benefits from excellent documentation, a large community of developers, and strong support from Microsoft. There are numerous resources available for beginners to learn and get help.

o **Great tooling with Visual Studio**: Visual Studio is one of the most powerful Integrated Development Environments (IDEs) for C#. It provides excellent debugging tools, code completion, and IntelliSense features, making it easier for beginners to write and troubleshoot code.

4. **Introduction to the .NET Framework** The .NET Framework is a comprehensive development platform for building a wide variety of applications. C# is deeply integrated with the .NET Framework, which provides a large

set of libraries for tasks like database interaction, file I/O, networking, and much more. The .NET framework helps developers build applications that are platform-independent and run on Windows, macOS, and Linux (via .NET Core, which is now part of .NET 5+).

Key components of the .NET Framework include:

- o **Common Language Runtime (CLR)**: The runtime environment that manages the execution of code, including memory management and garbage collection.
- o **Base Class Library (BCL)**: A collection of pre-written code that provides fundamental functionality, such as collections, string manipulation, file handling, and more.
- o **ASP.NET**: A framework for building dynamic web applications.
- o **Windows Forms and WPF (Windows Presentation Foundation)**: Frameworks for building rich desktop applications.

By using C# with the .NET framework, developers can quickly build robust, scalable, and maintainable applications.

5. **Introduction to Visual Studio** Visual Studio is an integrated development environment (IDE) from Microsoft

that provides developers with everything they need to build software with C#. It features advanced debugging, code completion, and project management tools, making it one of the most popular tools for C# development.

Visual Studio is particularly suited for Windows application development, offering extensive support for Windows Forms, WPF, and other Microsoft technologies. It also supports web and mobile application development, including ASP.NET and Xamarin projects.

Visual Studio has both a free community edition and more advanced paid versions with additional features for enterprise-level development.

Real-World Example: A Simple "Hello, World!" Console Application

The "Hello, World!" program is the most basic program that outputs a greeting message to the user. It serves as a great starting point for learning the syntax and structure of a C# program.

Steps:

1. **Open Visual Studio** and create a new **Console App (.NET Core)** project.

2. Name the project "HelloWorld" and select the **Create** button.

3. Visual Studio will generate a basic template for you. Replace the default code in the Program.cs file with the following:

```csharp
using System;

class Program
{
    static void Main(string[] args)
    {
        // Output Hello, World! to the console
        Console.WriteLine("Hello, World!");
    }
}
```

4. **Explanation of the Code**:

   o using System;: This line allows you to use the classes and methods from the System namespace, which includes the Console class.

   o class Program: Defines a class named Program. In C#, every application must have a class to define its structure.

   o static void Main(string[] args): This is the entry point of the program. The Main method is called when the application starts running.

- o Console.WriteLine("Hello, World!");: This line outputs the string "Hello, World!" to the console. The WriteLine method of the Console class writes the specified text to the console window.

5. **Run the Program**:
   - o Press **F5** or click the **Start** button to run the program. You should see the text "Hello, World!" displayed in the console window.

Real-World Use Case:

Although a "Hello, World!" program is simple, it forms the foundation of almost all applications. From here, you can build more complex applications by adding more features and functionality. For instance, after mastering basic syntax, you can create a basic calculator, a simple text-based game, or a small task management application.

Chapter 2: Setting Up Your Development Environment

Topics:

1. **Installing Visual Studio** Visual Studio is the most commonly used IDE for C# development. It is feature-rich, providing debugging, code completion, and version control integration. Here's how to install it and get started:

   o **Step 1: Download Visual Studio**
   Go to the <u>official Visual Studio download page</u> and choose the version suited for you. For beginners, the **Community Edition** is free and offers all the essential tools needed for C# development.

   o **Step 2: Run the Installer**
   Once the installer is downloaded, run it. You will be presented with several installation options. For C# development, select the **.NET Desktop Development** workload. This will install everything needed to work with C# on Windows Forms and Console Applications.

   o **Step 3: Complete the Installation**
   After selecting the required components, click **Install** and wait for the process to finish. The

installation time may vary depending on your internet speed and system performance.

- o **Step 4: Launch Visual Studio** Once installation is complete, launch Visual Studio. The first time you run it, you may be asked to sign in with a Microsoft account. You can skip this step if you don't have one or prefer not to log in.

2. **Setting Up the C# Environment** After Visual Studio is installed, it automatically configures the environment for C# development if you selected the appropriate workload during installation. Here's how to verify that everything is set up correctly:

    - o **Check C# Version**: Open Visual Studio and create a new C# project. By default, Visual Studio should use the latest stable version of C#. If you'd like to verify or update the version, you can check the **Tools** menu, select **Options**, and navigate to the **Projects and Solutions > .NET Core** section.

    - o **Set Up .NET SDK**: If you haven't installed the .NET SDK (which provides tools for building .NET apps), go to the official .NET download page and download the appropriate version for your operating system.

Visual Studio should automatically detect the .NET SDK once it's installed.

3. **Understanding the IDE (Integrated Development Environment)** Visual Studio is a powerful IDE that allows you to manage, write, test, and debug C# code all in one place. Let's explore some key features of the IDE:

- **Solution** **Explorer**: Located on the right side of the screen, this panel displays the structure of your project. It shows all files in your project, including code files, resources, and references.
- **Editor** **Window**: The central area where you write and edit code. Visual Studio's editor supports syntax highlighting, code completion, and error checking, which helps you write C# code quickly and accurately.
- **Toolbar**: The toolbar at the top provides quick access to common actions like building the project, running the application, and debugging.
- **Output** **Window**: This window displays important information, including build messages, debug information, and any errors or warnings in your code.

- o **Properties** **Window**:
  Located at the bottom-right, this window shows the properties of the selected object or item. For example, when you select a button in a Windows Forms application, the properties window lets you modify properties like the button's text, color, or size.

4. **Creating a New C# Project** To begin writing C# code, you need to create a new project. Follow these steps to create your first C# application:

   - o **Step 1: Open Visual Studio and Create a New Project**
     When Visual Studio starts, click on **Create a new project**. You will be prompted to choose the type of application you want to create.

   - o **Step 2: Choose a Template**
     Select **Console App (.NET Core)** or **Console App (.NET Framework)** depending on the version you want to use. The .NET Core version is the recommended choice as it is cross-platform and the most modern. Click **Next**.

   - o **Step 3: Configure the Project**
     Enter a name for your project, such as "MyFirstCSharpApp," and choose a location to save it. Click **Create**.

- **Step 4: Write Your Code**
  Visual Studio will automatically create a basic program with a Main method, which serves as the entry point for the application. You can now start writing code inside this method.

- **Step 5: Run Your Project**
  Press **F5** or click the **Start** button (green triangle) to run your application. If everything is set up correctly, the application will run, and you will see the output in the console window.

Real-World Example: Walkthrough of Setting Up a C# Project and Running the First Application

Let's walk through the process of setting up your first C# project from scratch and running a basic application that outputs a message to the console.

1. **Open Visual Studio** and create a new **Console App (.NET Core)** project.
   - Select **File > New > Project**.
   - Choose **Console App (.NET Core)** as the project template.

    o Name the project "MyFirstCSharpApp" and click **Create**.

2. **Write   Your   First   Program**

Visual Studio will generate a Program.cs file with a Main method. In this method, replace the existing code with:

csharp

```
using System;

class Program
{
    static void Main(string[] args)
    {
        Console.WriteLine("Welcome to C#! This is my first C# application.");
    }
}
```

This code uses Console.WriteLine to print a message to the console. The using System; at the top allows you to use the Console class from the System namespace.

3. **Run the Application**

    o Press **F5** or click the **Start** button to compile and run the application.

    o You should see the message "Welcome to C#! This is my first C# application." displayed in the console window.

Real-World Use Case

This simple example shows the foundational process of creating, writing, and running a C# application. In real-world applications, this process is the basis for creating complex software systems. For example, after mastering basic console applications, you could build a task management application, a personal finance tool, or even a small game. Each of these applications would start with the same process of setting up the project and writing code to accomplish specific tasks.

This chapter has equipped you with the tools to set up your development environment and run your first C# application. In subsequent chapters, we will delve deeper into coding techniques and building more sophisticated applications.

Chapter 3: Basic Syntax and Structure

Topics:

1. **Understanding Variables and Data Types** In C#, variables are used to store data that can be accessed and modified throughout the program. Each variable in C# is assigned a **data type**, which defines the kind of data it can hold (such as numbers, text, or boolean values).

   Common Data Types in C#:

   - **int**: Represents integers (whole numbers).
     Example: int number = 10;
   - **double**: Represents floating-point numbers (decimals).
     Example: double price = 19.99;
   - **bool**: Represents boolean values (true or false).
     Example: bool isActive = true;
   - **char**: Represents a single character.
     Example: char grade = 'A';
   - **string**: Represents a sequence of characters (text).
     Example: string message = "Hello, World!";

   Variable Declaration and Initialization: To declare a variable in C#, you need to specify its data type and name.

Optionally, you can initialize the variable by assigning a value:

csharp

```
int age = 25;
string name = "Alice";
double salary = 55000.75;
bool isEmployed = true;
```

2. **Basic Syntax in C#**

- o **Semicolons**: Every statement in C# ends with a semicolon (;).
- o **Curly Braces**: Blocks of code (like the body of a method or loop) are enclosed in curly braces ({ }).
- o **Comments**: Comments are used to explain code and are not executed. You can add comments using:
  - ▪ Single-line comments: // This is a comment
  - ▪ Multi-line comments: /* This is a comment block */

Example:

csharp

```
// This is a single-line comment
int number = 5;  // Declaring a variable
```

3. **Control Flow: Loops and Conditionals**

- o **Conditionals (if-else statements)**: Used to make decisions based on conditions.

  csharp

  ```csharp
  if (condition)
  {
      // Code to execute if the condition is true
  }
  else
  {
      // Code to execute if the condition is false
  }
  ```

  Example:

  csharp

  ```csharp
  if (age >= 18)
  {
      Console.WriteLine("You are an adult.");
  }
  else
  {
      Console.WriteLine("You are a minor.");
  }
  ```

- o **Loops**: Used to repeat a block of code multiple times.
  - ▪ **for loop**: Used when you know the number of iterations in advance.

csharp

```
for (int i = 0; i < 5; i++)
{
    Console.WriteLine(i);
}
```

- **while loop**: Runs as long as a condition is true.

csharp

```
int i = 0;
while (i < 5)
{
    Console.WriteLine(i);
    i++;
}
```

4. **Real-World Example: Writing a Program that Checks if a Number is Even or Odd** This program demonstrates how to use basic syntax, variables, and conditionals to check if a given number is even or odd.

Steps:

0.   The program will ask the user to input a number.

1.   It will check if the number is divisible by 2 (i.e., even) or not (i.e., odd).

2. It will print the result to the console.

Code:

csharp

```csharp
using System;

class Program
{
    static void Main(string[] args)
    {
        // Step 1: Ask the user for a number
        Console.Write("Enter a number: ");
        int number = Convert.ToInt32(Console.ReadLine());

        // Step 2: Check if the number is even or odd
        if (number % 2 == 0)
        {
            // Step 3: If the number is divisible by 2, it's even
            Console.WriteLine("The number is even.");
        }
        else
        {
            // If the number is not divisible by 2, it's odd
            Console.WriteLine("The number is odd.");
        }
    }
}
```

Explanation:

- o Console.Write: Displays a message without a newline.
- o Convert.ToInt32(Console.ReadLine()): Reads user input from the console and converts it into an integer.
- o number % 2: The modulus operator (%) returns the remainder of the division of number by 2. If the result is 0, the number is even; otherwise, it is odd.
- o The if-else statement checks whether the remainder is 0 or not, and outputs whether the number is even or odd.

5. **Testing the Program**
   - o When you run the program, you will be prompted to enter a number.
   - o If you input 4, the program will output "The number is even."
   - o If you input 7, the program will output "The number is odd."

Real-World Use Case

This basic "even or odd" program can be a starting point for more complex applications, such as:

- **Number guessing games** where you check if a guessed number is within a range.

- **Validating user input** for other numerical conditions (e.g., checking if a number is positive or negative).
- **Building calculators** that perform different operations based on user input.

The concepts of using variables, conditionals, and loops form the core foundation of many real-world programs, from simple utilities to complex systems. Understanding these basic structures is essential for writing effective C# code.

Chapter 4: Control Flow: If-Else Statements and Switch

Topics:

1. **Introduction to Conditionals** Conditionals are used in programming to make decisions based on whether certain conditions are true or false. In C#, the most common conditional statements are **if**, **else**, and **switch**. These statements allow you to control the flow of your program based on different conditions and inputs.

   o **If Statement**: Used to execute a block of code only if a specified condition is true.

   o **Else Statement**: Used in conjunction with an if statement to execute a block of code if the if condition is false.

   o **Else-If Statement**: Used to specify additional conditions to check if the initial if condition is false.

   o **Switch Statement**: Used when you need to evaluate a variable against multiple possible values and execute different blocks of code depending on which value matches.

2. **If-Else Statements** An **if-else** statement allows you to execute different code blocks based on whether a condition evaluates to true or false. The syntax is as follows:

csharp

```
if (condition)
{
    // Code to execute if the condition is true
}
else
{
    // Code to execute if the condition is false
}
```

- o **Example of an If-Else Statement**:

csharp

```
int age = 20;
if (age >= 18)
{
    Console.WriteLine("You are an adult.");
}
else
{
    Console.WriteLine("You are a minor.");
}
```

3. **Switch Statements** A **switch** statement is used when you have a variable that can take multiple discrete values and you need to execute different blocks of code based on the value of that variable. It's more efficient and readable than using

multiple if-else statements when you are dealing with multiple conditions.

The syntax for a switch statement is:

csharp

```
switch (variable)
{
    case value1:
        // Code to execute if variable equals value1
        break;
    case value2:
        // Code to execute if variable equals value2
        break;
    default:
        // Code to execute if no case matches
        break;
}
```

- o **Example of a Switch Statement**:

    csharp

    ```
    int dayOfWeek = 3;
    switch (dayOfWeek)
    {
        case 1:
            Console.WriteLine("Monday");
            break;
    ```

```
        case 2:
            Console.WriteLine("Tuesday");
            break;
        case 3:
            Console.WriteLine("Wednesday");
            break;
        default:
            Console.WriteLine("Invalid day");
            break;
    }
```

In the example, the program checks the value of dayOfWeek and prints the corresponding day of the week. If no case matches, it will print "Invalid day."

4. **Real-World Example: A Simple User Authentication Program** Let's create a simple user authentication program using if-else and switch statements. The program will check if the entered username and password match the stored credentials and provide access accordingly.

Steps:

- o The program will ask the user for their username and password.
- o It will check if the provided username and password match predefined values.
- o Based on the check, the program will either grant access or deny it.

Code:

```csharp
csharp

using System;

class Program
{
    static void Main(string[] args)
    {
        // Predefined credentials
        string storedUsername = "admin";
        string storedPassword = "password123";

        // Ask for username and password
        Console.Write("Enter username: ");
        string username = Console.ReadLine();

        Console.Write("Enter password: ");
        string password = Console.ReadLine();

        // Authenticate user using if-else
        if (username == storedUsername && password == storedPassword)
        {
            Console.WriteLine("Access granted.");
        }
        else
        {
            Console.WriteLine("Invalid credentials. Access denied.");
        }
```

```csharp
// Switch Example: Role-based access
Console.Write("Enter your role (Admin/User): ");
string role = Console.ReadLine();

switch (role.ToLower())
{
    case "admin":
        Console.WriteLine("Welcome, Admin! You have full access.");
        break;
    case "user":
        Console.WriteLine("Welcome, User! You have limited access.");
        break;
    default:
        Console.WriteLine("Invalid role.");
        break;
    }
  }
}
```

Explanation:

○ The program first prompts the user to enter their username and password.

○ It uses an if-else statement to check if the entered credentials match the predefined storedUsername and storedPassword. If they match, it grants access; otherwise, it denies access.

- o After authentication, the program prompts the user to enter their role (either "Admin" or "User").
- o The switch statement evaluates the role and prints a corresponding message. If the entered role is invalid, the program prints "Invalid role."

5. **Testing the Program**

- o When you run the program, it will first prompt you for a username and password. If you enter "admin" and "password123", you will get "Access granted."
- o After entering your role, if you enter "admin", the program will display "Welcome, Admin! You have full access." If you enter "user", it will display "Welcome, User! You have limited access."
- o If the role entered is neither "admin" nor "user", the program will display "Invalid role."

Real-World Use Case

This user authentication program is a basic example of how conditionals are used in real-world applications. In more complex systems, you can extend this concept to:

- • **Role-based access control** in web applications (e.g., Admin, Editor, Viewer).

- **Login systems** where user credentials are stored in databases and retrieved for validation.
- **Authorization systems** where different actions or features are granted based on the user's role (e.g., a regular user versus a moderator).

The concepts of if-else and switch statements are essential for handling decision-making processes, validating inputs, and controlling the flow of a program, making them fundamental building blocks for any real-world application.

Chapter 5: Loops and Iteration

Topics:

1. **Introduction to Loops** Loops are essential structures in programming that allow you to repeat a block of code multiple times. In C#, there are three main types of loops: **for**, **while**, and **do-while**. Each loop has its own specific use cases, and understanding how to use them is crucial for efficient coding and iteration.

   o **For Loop**: A for loop is used when you know how many times you need to repeat a block of code. It's ideal for situations where you can define a starting point, an ending point, and an increment/decrement.

   Syntax:

   csharp

   ```csharp
   for (initialization; condition; increment/decrement)
   {
       // Code to execute
   }
   ```

   ▪ **Example**:

   csharp

   ```csharp
   for (int i = 0; i < 5; i++)
   ```

```
{
    Console.WriteLine(i);  // Prints 0 to 4
}
```

Explanation:

- The loop starts by initializing i to 0.
- The loop will continue as long as i is less than 5.
- After each iteration, i is incremented by 1.

o **While Loop**: A while loop continues executing the block of code as long as the specified condition evaluates to true. The condition is checked before the code block runs.

Syntax:

csharp

```
while (condition)
{
    // Code to execute
}
```

- **Example**:

csharp

```
int i = 0;
while (i < 5)
```

```
{
    Console.WriteLine(i);  // Prints 0 to 4
    i++;  // Increment i by 1
}
```

Explanation:

- The condition i < 5 is checked before each iteration.
- The loop runs as long as the condition is true.
  - **Do-While Loop**: A do-while loop is similar to a while loop, except that it guarantees at least one iteration of the code block, because the condition is checked **after** the code block runs.

Syntax:

csharp

```
do
{
    // Code to execute
} while (condition);
```

- **Example**:

csharp

```
int i = 0;
do
```

```
        {
            Console.WriteLine(i);  // Prints 0 to 4
            i++;
        } while (i < 5);
```

Explanation:

- The code inside the loop is executed first, and then the condition is checked. The loop continues as long as the condition is true.

2. **Iteration Techniques** Iteration techniques are strategies for efficiently accessing and manipulating collections of data. Some common iteration techniques include:

   o **For-each loop**: An alternative to traditional loops that iterates over each element of a collection (like arrays, lists, etc.) without the need to manually manage the index. **Syntax:**

   csharp

   ```
   foreach (var element in collection)
   {
       // Code to execute for each element
   }
   ```

   Example:

   csharp

   ```
   int[] numbers = { 1, 2, 3, 4, 5 };
   foreach (int number in numbers)
   ```

```
{
    Console.WriteLine(number);  // Prints 1 to 5
}
```

- o **Nested Loops**: A loop inside another loop. Nested loops are useful for working with multi-dimensional data structures like 2D arrays. **Example**:

csharp

```
for (int i = 0; i < 3; i++)
{
    for (int j = 0; j < 3; j++)
    {
        Console.WriteLine($"i: {i}, j: {j}");
    }
}
```

Real-World Example: A Program to Find the Sum of an Array of Numbers

In this example, we will use a loop to find the sum of all elements in an array of integers. This demonstrates how to iterate through a collection (in this case, an array) and perform a calculation.

Steps:

1. Declare an array of integers.

2. Use a loop to iterate through each element of the array and add it to a running total (sum).

3. Display the final sum to the user.

Code:

csharp

```csharp
using System;

class Program
{
    static void Main(string[] args)
    {
        // Step 1: Declare and initialize the array
        int[] numbers = { 10, 20, 30, 40, 50 };

        // Step 2: Initialize a variable to hold the sum
        int sum = 0;

        // Step 3: Use a loop to iterate through the array and calculate the sum
        foreach (int number in numbers)
        {
            sum += number;  // Add each number to sum
        }

        // Step 4: Display the sum
        Console.WriteLine("The sum of the array elements is: " + sum);
    }
}
```

Explanation:

- **Array Initialization**: The array numbers contains five integers: 10, 20, 30, 40, and 50.
- **For-each Loop**: The foreach loop iterates through each element in the numbers array. On each iteration, the number variable holds the current element, and sum += number adds the current number to the sum variable.
- **Result**: After the loop finishes, the sum variable holds the total of all the elements in the array. The program then prints the result to the console.

Output:

python

The sum of the array elements is: 150

Real-World Use Case

This simple example of calculating the sum of an array can be expanded into more complex scenarios, such as:

- **Calculating averages**: You can modify the program to find the average of an array by dividing the sum by the number of elements.

- **Finding the maximum or minimum value**: You could adapt the program to find the highest or lowest number in an array by comparing each element during iteration.

- **Processing user input**: The program could be extended to take an array of numbers as user input, allowing dynamic calculations.

In real-world applications, you frequently need to loop through collections of data, whether it's processing lists of items, iterating over rows in a database, or analyzing data from a file. Mastering loops and iteration techniques is fundamental to being an effective C# programmer.

Chapter 6: Methods and Functions

Topics:

1. **Creating and Using Functions** Functions (or methods in C# terminology) are blocks of reusable code that perform specific tasks. They allow you to organize your code more efficiently and avoid repeating yourself. Functions help with breaking down complex problems into smaller, more manageable tasks.

   Syntax for Defining a Method:

   csharp

   ```
   returnType MethodName(parameters)
   {
      // Method body
   }
   ```

   - o **returnType**: The type of data that the method will return (e.g., int, void, string, etc.). If the method doesn't return any value, use void.
   - o **MethodName**: The name of the method that is used to call it.
   - o **parameters**: Optional values that the method can accept to work with (e.g., numbers, strings).

Example:

csharp

```
int Add(int a, int b)  // Method that takes two integers and returns an integer
{
    return a + b;
}
```

Calling a Method:

csharp

```
int result = Add(5, 3);  // Calls the Add method and stores the result
```

2. **Understanding Method Parameters** Parameters are variables used to pass data into a method. When defining a method, you can specify parameters that allow the method to work with data passed to it at runtime.

   o **Value Parameters**: These parameters are passed by value, meaning the method gets a copy of the value and cannot change the original variable.

   o **Reference Parameters**: These parameters are passed by reference, meaning changes made inside the method will affect the original variable. **Syntax**:

   csharp

   ```
   void UpdateValue(ref int num)
   ```

```
{
    num = num + 5;
}
```

3. **Example**:

4. csharp

5.

6. void PrintMessage(string message) // Accepts a string parameter

7. {

8.   Console.WriteLine(message);

9. }

10. **Return Types** The **return type** of a method defines the kind of data the method will return after execution. If a method doesn't need to return any value, you can use void as the return type.

   o **Example with return type**:

   csharp

   ```
   int Multiply(int a, int b)
   {
       return a * b;
   }
   ```

   o **Calling a method with a return type**:

   csharp

   ```
   int result = Multiply(5, 3); // The method returns a value, which
   is stored in the result
   ```

11. When you call a method with a return type, you can use the returned value directly in expressions, store it in variables, or perform calculations.

Real-World Example: A Program that Calculates the Factorial of a Number

Factorial is a common mathematical operation where the factorial of a number n is the product of all positive integers less than or equal to n. It is denoted as n!.

Formula:

scss

$n! = n * (n-1) * (n-2) * \ldots * 1$

For example:

- $5! = 5 * 4 * 3 * 2 * 1 = 120$
- $4! = 4 * 3 * 2 * 1 = 24$

We will create a method to calculate the factorial of a number using both an iterative and a recursive approach.

Step-by-Step Approach:

1. **Define the Factorial Method**: The method will take an integer as a parameter, calculate its factorial, and return the result.

2. **Calling the Method**: The user will input a number, and the program will display the factorial of that number.

Code:

csharp

```csharp
using System;

class Program
{
    // Method to calculate factorial using iteration
    static int CalculateFactorial(int n)
    {
        int factorial = 1;
        for (int i = 1; i <= n; i++)
        {
            factorial *= i;
        }
        return factorial;
    }

    // Optional: Recursive method to calculate factorial
    static int RecursiveFactorial(int n)
    {
        if (n == 0 || n == 1)
            return 1;  // Base case
```

```csharp
        else
            return n * RecursiveFactorial(n - 1);  // Recursive call
    }


    static void Main(string[] args)
    {
        // Ask the user to input a number
        Console.Write("Enter a number to calculate its factorial: ");
        int number = Convert.ToInt32(Console.ReadLine());

        // Call the method to calculate the factorial
        int result = CalculateFactorial(number);

        // Display the result
        Console.WriteLine($"The factorial of {number} is: {result}");

        // Optional: Display the result using the recursive method
        int recursiveResult = RecursiveFactorial(number);
        Console.WriteLine($"Using recursion, the factorial of {number} is:
{recursiveResult}");
    }
}
```

Explanation:

- **CalculateFactorial Method**: This method calculates the factorial iteratively. It uses a for loop to multiply all integers from 1 to n.

- **RecursiveFactorial Method**: This method calculates the factorial recursively. It calls itself with n-1 until n reaches 1, at which point it returns 1 (base case).
- **Calling the Method**: In the Main method, the program prompts the user to input a number, then calculates and displays the factorial of that number using both the iterative and recursive methods.

Output Example:

vbnet

Enter a number to calculate its factorial: 5
The factorial of 5 is: 120
Using recursion, the factorial of 5 is: 120

Real-World Use Case

The concept of calculating the factorial of a number is often used in fields like combinatorics, probability, and mathematics in general. Some real-world use cases for factorials in programming include:

- **Combinatorics**: Calculating permutations and combinations.
- **Algorithm Analysis**: Factorials are used in the analysis of certain algorithms, especially those with recursive or combinatorial behavior.

- **Data Science**: Factorials are important for calculating probabilities, particularly in statistical models.

Mastering functions and methods, along with understanding how to pass parameters and handle return types, is key to building organized, reusable, and maintainable code in C#. This chapter gives you a foundation in writing methods that make your programs modular and efficient.

Chapter 7: Object-Oriented Programming (OOP) Fundamentals

Topics:

1. **Introduction to Object-Oriented Programming (OOP)**

   Object-Oriented Programming (OOP) is a programming paradigm that organizes software design around **objects** rather than functions and logic. In OOP, objects represent entities that combine both **state** (data) and **behavior** (methods or functions). OOP allows you to create modular, reusable, and maintainable code. It is based on the following core principles:

   - **Classes**: A class is a blueprint or template for creating objects. It defines the properties and methods that an object can have.

   - **Objects**: An object is an instance of a class. It holds data (properties) and can perform actions (methods) based on its class definition.

   - **Methods**: Methods define the behavior of objects and are functions that belong to a class. They perform operations on the object's data.

   - **Encapsulation**: The bundling of data (properties) and methods that operate on that data into a single unit (class). It also involves restricting direct access to some of an object's components, which is achieved through access modifiers (e.g., public, private).

- o **Inheritance**: Inheritance allows a class to inherit the properties and methods of another class, promoting code reuse.

- o **Polymorphism**: Polymorphism allows different classes to implement methods in ways that are specific to them, even though they share the same method name.

- o **Abstraction**: Abstraction involves simplifying complex systems by providing a clear and concise interface while hiding unnecessary implementation details.

2. **Classes and Objects**

- o **Class**: A class is defined using the class keyword and serves as a blueprint for creating objects. It can contain properties (variables) and methods (functions).

- o **Object**: An object is an instance of a class. Once a class is defined, you can create multiple objects based on that class.

Syntax:

csharp

```
class ClassName
{
    // Properties (Fields)
    public int property1;
    public string property2;

    // Method
    public void MethodName()
    {
        // Method code here
    }
}
```

Creating an Object:

csharp

```
ClassName objectName = new ClassName();
```

Example:

csharp

```
class Car
{
    // Properties
    public string Make;
    public string Model;
    public int Year;
    public string Color;

    // Method to display car details
```

```csharp
    public void DisplayCarInfo()
    {
        Console.WriteLine($"Car Info: {Year} {Make} {Model} ({Color})");
    }
}
```

```csharp
// Creating an object of the Car class
Car myCar = new Car();
myCar.Make = "Toyota";
myCar.Model = "Corolla";
myCar.Year = 2021;
myCar.Color = "Red";
```

```csharp
// Calling the method on the object
myCar.DisplayCarInfo();
```

Explanation:

- o   Car is the class, and it defines four properties (Make, Model, Year, Color) and a method (DisplayCarInfo).
- o   The DisplayCarInfo method prints out the car's details.
- o   An object myCar is created from the Car class and its properties are set.
- o   The DisplayCarInfo method is called to display the car's details.

3.   **Access Modifiers** Access modifiers define the visibility and accessibility of class members (properties and methods). Common modifiers include:

- o   public: The member is accessible from anywhere.

- o   private: The member is only accessible within the class.

- o   protected: The member is accessible within the class and derived classes.

- o   internal: The member is accessible within the same assembly.

Example:

csharp

```
class Car
{
    private string make;
    public string Model;
    public int Year;

    public void SetMake(string carMake)
    {
        make = carMake;  // Using a method to set the private property
    }

    public void DisplayCarInfo()
    {
        Console.WriteLine($"Car Info: {make} {Model} ({Year})");
    }
}
```

```csharp
Car myCar = new Car();
myCar.SetMake("Honda");
myCar.Model = "Civic";
myCar.Year = 2020;
myCar.DisplayCarInfo();  // Displays "Car Info: Honda Civic (2020)"
```

Real-World Example: A Basic "Car" Class with Properties and Methods

In this example, we will define a Car class with several properties (such as Make, Model, Year, and Color) and a method that allows us to display the car's details. This will demonstrate how to use classes, objects, and methods in a simple real-world scenario.

Steps:

1. Define a Car class with properties.
2. Define a method within the class to display the car's details.
3. Create an object (instance) of the Car class and assign values to its properties.
4. Call the method to display the car's details.

Code:

csharp

using System;

```csharp
class Car
{
    // Properties of the Car class
    public string Make;
    public string Model;
    public int Year;
    public string Color;

    // Constructor to initialize the Car object
    public Car(string make, string model, int year, string color)
    {
        Make = make;
        Model = model;
        Year = year;
        Color = color;
    }

    // Method to display car details
    public void DisplayCarInfo()
    {
        Console.WriteLine($"Car Info: {Year} {Make} {Model} ({Color})");
    }

    // Method to start the car
    public void StartCar()
    {
        Console.WriteLine("The car has started.");
    }

    // Method to stop the car
```

```csharp
    public void StopCar()
    {
        Console.WriteLine("The car has stopped.");
    }
}

class Program
{
    static void Main(string[] args)
    {
        // Create a new Car object using the constructor
        Car myCar = new Car("Ford", "Mustang", 2021, "Blue");

        // Call methods on the Car object
        myCar.DisplayCarInfo();  // Displays: Car Info: 2021 Ford Mustang (Blue)
        myCar.StartCar();        // Displays: The car has started.
        myCar.StopCar();         // Displays: The car has stopped.
    }
}
```

Explanation:

- **Car Class**:
    - The Car class has four properties: Make, Model, Year, and Color.
    - A **constructor** (public Car(...)) is used to initialize a new Car object with the specified values for these properties.
    - Three methods are defined:

- DisplayCarInfo() prints the details of the car.
- StartCar() simulates starting the car.
- StopCar() simulates stopping the car.

- **Program Class**:
  - Inside the Main method, we create an object myCar from the Car class, passing values for Make, Model, Year, and Color through the constructor.
  - We then call the DisplayCarInfo(), StartCar(), and StopCar() methods on the myCar object.

Output:

yaml

Car Info: 2021 Ford Mustang (Blue)
The car has started.
The car has stopped.

Real-World Use Case

This basic Car class can be extended to represent more complex systems, such as:

- **Inventory Management Systems**: The Car class could be used in a car dealership's system to represent different car models, with methods to check car availability, calculate prices, or manage maintenance schedules.

- **Simulation Applications**: The Car class could be part of a simulation game where you model vehicles and their behavior.
- **Fleet Management**: A Fleet class could be created to manage a collection of Car objects, with methods to add, remove, and track the status of each car in the fleet.

In all these cases, using classes and objects allows you to manage real-world entities more efficiently, making your code more modular, reusable, and maintainable.

Chapter 8: Working with Strings

Topics:

1. **String Manipulation in C#** Strings are sequences of characters and are one of the most frequently used data types in programming. In C#, strings are immutable, meaning once a string is created, it cannot be changed directly. However, you can manipulate strings using various built-in methods that return modified copies of the original string.

   Common String Operations:

   o **Concatenation**: Joining two or more strings together.

   csharp

   ```
   string fullName = "John" + " " + "Doe";  // Concatenates "John"
   and "Doe"
   ```

   o **Interpolation**: A more readable way of concatenating strings by embedding expressions directly within a string.

   csharp

   ```
   string firstName = "John";
   string lastName = "Doe";
   ```

```csharp
string fullName = $"{firstName} {lastName}";   // Uses interpolation
```

- **String Length**: The Length property returns the number of characters in a string.

csharp

```csharp
string name = "John";
int length = name.Length;  // length will be 4
```

- **Accessing Characters**: You can access individual characters in a string by their index (starting from 0).

csharp

```csharp
char firstLetter = name[0];  // 'J'
```

2. **Common String Methods** C# provides several methods for manipulating strings. Some of the most commonly used methods are:

- **ToLower()**: Converts a string to lowercase.

csharp

```csharp
string text = "HELLO";
string lowerText = text.ToLower();  // "hello"
```

- **ToUpper()**: Converts a string to uppercase.

csharp

```
string text = "hello";
string upperText = text.ToUpper();  // "HELLO"
```

o **Trim()**: Removes leading and trailing whitespace from a string.

csharp

```
string text = "  hello  ";
string trimmedText = text.Trim();  // "hello"
```

o **Substring()**: Extracts a part of the string.

csharp

```
string text = "Hello, World!";
string subText = text.Substring(7, 5);  // "World"
```

o **Replace()**: Replaces all occurrences of a substring with another substring.

csharp

```
string text = "I love apples";
string replacedText = text.Replace("apples", "oranges");  // "I love oranges"
```

- o **Split()**: Splits a string into an array based on a delimiter.

csharp

```
string text = "apple,orange,banana";
string[] fruits = text.Split(','); // ["apple", "orange", "banana"]
```

- o **Contains()**: Checks if a string contains a specified substring.

csharp

```
string text = "Hello, World!";
bool hasWorld = text.Contains("World"); // true
```

3. **String Formatting** String formatting allows you to create strings in a structured way by embedding values into a template. C# provides several ways to format strings:

- o **String Concatenation**: Using the + operator to join strings.

csharp

```
string name = "John";
int age = 30;
string formattedString = "Name: " + name + ", Age: " + age; // Concatenation
```

- **String Interpolation**: A cleaner and more readable way to format strings using the $ symbol.

  csharp

  ```
  string name = "John";
  int age = 30;
  string formattedString = $"Name: {name}, Age: {age}";  // String Interpolation
  ```

- **String.Format()**: Allows formatting of strings with placeholders {0}, {1}, etc.

  csharp

  ```
  string formattedString = string.Format("Name: {0}, Age: {1}", "John", 30); // String.Format()
  ```

- **ToString()**: You can call ToString() on different types to convert them to a string in a specific format.

  csharp

  ```
  double number = 1234.5678;
  string formattedNumber = number.ToString("C");  // "$1,234.57" (Currency format)
  ```

73

Real-World Example: A Program that Parses and Formats User Input into a Standard Format

In this example, we will write a program that asks the user to input their full name and date of birth. The program will then format the name in title case (first letter of each word capitalized) and format the date of birth in a specific format (e.g., "MM/dd/yyyy").

Steps:

1. The program will prompt the user for their full name and birth date.
2. The program will convert the name to title case (e.g., "john doe" → "John Doe").
3. The program will parse and format the date of birth into the "MM/dd/yyyy" format.

Code:

csharp

```
using System;

class Program
{
    static void Main(string[] args)
    {
        // Step 1: Ask for user's full name
        Console.Write("Enter your full name: ");
```

```
        string fullName = Console.ReadLine();


        // Step 2: Convert name to title case (each word capitalized)
        string formattedName = ToTitleCase(fullName);
        Console.WriteLine($"Formatted Name: {formattedName}");


        // Step 3: Ask for user's date of birth
        Console.Write("Enter your date of birth (MM/dd/yyyy): ");
        string dobInput = Console.ReadLine();


        // Step 4: Parse and format the date
        DateTime dob = DateTime.ParseExact(dobInput, "MM/dd/yyyy", null);
        string formattedDob = dob.ToString("MMMM dd, yyyy");
        Console.WriteLine($"Formatted Date of Birth: {formattedDob}");
    }


    // Method to convert name to title case
    static string ToTitleCase(string name)
    {
        // Convert each word to title case (first letter uppercase, rest lowercase)
        TextInfo  textInfo  =  new  System.Globalization.CultureInfo("en-US",
false).TextInfo;
        return textInfo.ToTitleCase(name.ToLower());
    }
}
```

Explanation:

1. **Full Name Formatting**:

- o The program asks the user for their full name and converts it to title case using the ToTitleCase() method. This method ensures that the first letter of each word is capitalized, while the rest of the letters are in lowercase.
- o We use the TextInfo.ToTitleCase() method from System.Globalization to handle title casing.

2. **Date of Birth Parsing and Formatting**:
   - o The program asks the user for their date of birth in the format "MM/dd/yyyy".
   - o It parses the input string into a DateTime object using DateTime.ParseExact().
   - o Then, the date is formatted into a more readable format ("MMMM dd, yyyy") using ToString().

3. **Output**:
   - o The formatted name and formatted date of birth are displayed to the user.

Output Example:

yaml

Enter your full name: john doe
Formatted Name: John Doe
Enter your date of birth (MM/dd/yyyy): 12/15/1990
Formatted Date of Birth: December 15, 1990

Real-World Use Case

This string parsing and formatting process can be applied in various real-world scenarios, such as:

- **User Registration Systems**: Ensuring that user names are properly formatted and that dates are consistently displayed.
- **Data Validation**: Parsing and validating user inputs such as email addresses, phone numbers, and dates in a standardized format.
- **Reports and Invoices**: Formatting names and dates for generating professional-looking documents like invoices, receipts, and formal correspondence.

By mastering string manipulation and formatting, you can create robust and user-friendly applications that handle text data in a consistent and professional manner.

Chapter 9: Arrays and Collections

Topics:

1. **Using Arrays** An **array** is a fixed-size collection of elements of the same data type. Arrays allow you to store multiple values in a single variable, making it easier to manage related data.

   o **Declaring an Array**: You define an array by specifying the type of its elements followed by square brackets [].

   csharp

   ```
   int[] numbers = new int[5]; // Declares an array of 5 integers
   ```

   o **Initializing an Array**: You can initialize an array at the time of declaration or later.

   csharp

   ```
   int[] numbers = { 1, 2, 3, 4, 5 }; // Array with predefined values
   ```

   o **Accessing Array Elements**: You access array elements using an index, which starts at 0.

   csharp

   ```
   int firstNumber = numbers[0]; // Accesses the first element (1)
   ```

o **Array Length**: You can find the number of elements in an array using the Length property.

csharp

int length = numbers.Length; // Returns the length of the array

2. **Example**:
3. csharp
4.
5. int[] numbers = { 10, 20, 30, 40, 50 };
6. for (int i = 0; i < numbers.Length; i++)
7. {
8.   Console.WriteLine(numbers[i]); // Prints each number in the array
9. }
10. **Using Lists A List** is a dynamic collection that allows you to store elements of the same type, but unlike arrays, Lists can grow and shrink in size dynamically as elements are added or removed.

o **Declaring and Initializing a List**:

csharp

List<int> numbers = new List<int>();

You can add elements to a List using the Add() method:

csharp

```
numbers.Add(10);
numbers.Add(20);
```

o **Accessing List Elements**:

csharp

```
int firstNumber = numbers[0]; // Accesses the first element (10)
```

o **Removing Elements**:

csharp

```
numbers.Remove(10); // Removes the first occurrence of 10
numbers.RemoveAt(0); // Removes the element at index 0
```

o **List Methods**:

- **Add()**: Adds an element to the list.
- **Remove()**: Removes a specific element from the list.
- **Clear()**: Removes all elements from the list.
- **Contains()**: Checks if an element exists in the list.

Example:

csharp

```
List<string> names = new List<string>();
names.Add("Alice");
```

```
names.Add("Bob");
names.Add("Charlie");

foreach (var name in names)
{
    Console.WriteLine(name);  // Prints each name in the list
}
```

11. **Other Collections** Collections in C# are more advanced than arrays and Lists, offering greater flexibility. Common collections include:

    o **Dictionary**: A collection of key-value pairs.

    o **Queue**: A first-in, first-out (FIFO) collection.

    o **Stack**: A last-in, first-out (LIFO) collection.

    o **HashSet**: A collection that contains only unique elements.

    Example of Dictionary:

    csharp

```
Dictionary<int, string> contacts = new Dictionary<int, string>();
contacts.Add(1, "John Doe");
contacts.Add(2, "Jane Smith");

string contactName = contacts[1];  // Accesses the value by key
Console.WriteLine(contactName);    // Outputs "John Doe"
```

Real-World Example: A Program That Manages a List of Contacts

In this example, we will create a program that allows the user to manage a list of contacts. Each contact will have a name and phone number. The program will allow the user to add, remove, and display contacts.

Steps:

1. Define a class to represent a contact with a name and phone number.
2. Use a List<Contact> to store multiple contacts.
3. Provide methods to add, remove, and display contacts.

Code:

csharp

```
using System;
using System.Collections.Generic;

class Contact
{
    public string Name { get; set; }
    public string PhoneNumber { get; set; }

    public Contact(string name, string phoneNumber)
    {
```

```csharp
        Name = name;

        PhoneNumber = phoneNumber;

    }


    public void DisplayContactInfo()

    {

        Console.WriteLine($"Name: {Name}, Phone: {PhoneNumber}");

    }

}


class Program

{

    static void Main(string[] args)

    {

        List<Contact> contacts = new List<Contact>();


        // Adding some contacts

        contacts.Add(new Contact("John Doe", "555-1234"));

        contacts.Add(new Contact("Jane Smith", "555-5678"));

        contacts.Add(new Contact("Alice Johnson", "555-8765"));


        // Displaying all contacts

        Console.WriteLine("Contacts List:");

        foreach (var contact in contacts)

        {

            contact.DisplayContactInfo();

        }


        // Removing a contact

        Console.WriteLine("\nRemoving a contact...");
```

```
contacts.RemoveAt(1);  // Remove the second contact (Jane Smith)


// Displaying updated contacts list
Console.WriteLine("\nUpdated Contacts List:");
foreach (var contact in contacts)
{
   contact.DisplayContactInfo();
}


// Adding a new contact
contacts.Add(new Contact("Bob Brown", "555-4321"));


// Displaying all contacts again
Console.WriteLine("\nFinal Contacts List:");
foreach (var contact in contacts)
{
   contact.DisplayContactInfo();
}
   }
}
```

Explanation:

- **Contact Class**: The Contact class represents a contact with two properties: Name and PhoneNumber. It also has a method DisplayContactInfo() that prints out the contact's details.

- **Main Program**:
  - A List<Contact> is used to store the contacts.

- o The program adds three contacts to the list using the Add() method.
- o It then displays all the contacts using a foreach loop.
- o After that, it removes a contact using RemoveAt() and displays the updated list.
- o Finally, a new contact is added and the final list is displayed.

Output Example:

yaml

Contacts List:

Name: John Doe, Phone: 555-1234

Name: Jane Smith, Phone: 555-5678

Name: Alice Johnson, Phone: 555-8765

Removing a contact...

Updated Contacts List:

Name: John Doe, Phone: 555-1234

Name: Alice Johnson, Phone: 555-8765

Final Contacts List:

Name: John Doe, Phone: 555-1234

Name: Alice Johnson, Phone: 555-8765

Name: Bob Brown, Phone: 555-4321

Real-World Use Case

This contact management system can be expanded in several real-world scenarios:

- **Address Book**: A program for managing personal or business contacts.
- **Customer Relationship Management (CRM) System**: A larger system to manage client information, such as contact details, interaction history, and customer preferences.
- **Mobile or Desktop Applications**: Apps that store and organize user contact information for messaging, calling, or emailing.

By understanding how to work with arrays, Lists, and other collections in C#, you can effectively manage large sets of related data, making your programs more scalable and maintainable.

Chapter 10: Handling Exceptions

Topics:

1. **Understanding Exceptions** Exceptions are runtime errors
    that occur when something goes wrong during the execution
    of a program. These errors can cause a program to terminate
    unexpectedly unless they are handled properly. In C#,
    exceptions are objects that derive from the System.Exception
    class. They provide information about the error, such as its
    type, message, and stack trace.

    Why Handle Exceptions?

    o   **Graceful Error Handling**: Instead of crashing the
        program, exceptions allow you to handle errors
        gracefully, improving the user experience.
    o   **Debugging**: Handling exceptions helps to catch
        issues at runtime and log them for debugging
        purposes.
    o   **Preventing Program Crashes**: Without exception
        handling, errors might cause your program to
        terminate unexpectedly, which could result in data
        loss or user frustration.

2. **Using Try-Catch Blocks** The most common way to handle
    exceptions in C# is by using **try-catch** blocks. The try block

contains the code that might throw an exception, and the catch block handles the exception if it occurs.

Basic Syntax:

csharp

```
try
{
    // Code that may throw an exception
}
catch (ExceptionType ex)
{
    // Code to handle the exception
    Console.WriteLine(ex.Message); // Print the exception message
}
```

Example:

csharp

```
try
{
    int result = 10 / 0; // Division by zero will throw an exception
}
catch (DivideByZeroException ex)
{
    Console.WriteLine("Error: " + ex.Message); // Handle the specific exception
}
```

○ **Multiple Catch Blocks**: You can have multiple catch blocks to handle different types of exceptions.

csharp

```csharp
try
{
    // Code that may throw multiple types of exceptions
}
catch (FormatException ex)
{
    Console.WriteLine("Invalid format: " + ex.Message);
}
catch (ArgumentNullException ex)
{
    Console.WriteLine("Argument is null: " + ex.Message);
}
```

3. **Finally Block** The finally block, if present, is always executed regardless of whether an exception occurred or not. It is typically used for cleanup operations, such as closing files or releasing resources.

Syntax:

csharp

```csharp
try
{
    // Code that may throw an exception
```

```
}
catch (Exception ex)
{
    // Handle exception
}
finally
{
    // Cleanup code, always runs
}
```

Example:

csharp

```
try
{
    Console.WriteLine("Entering try block");
    int result = 10 / 0;  // This will throw a DivideByZeroException
}
catch (DivideByZeroException ex)
{
    Console.WriteLine("Error: " + ex.Message);
}
finally
{
    Console.WriteLine("Finally block executed");  // This will always run
}
```

4. **Exception Types** C# provides a variety of built-in exception types. Some common ones include:

    o   DivideByZeroException: Thrown when dividing by zero.

- o FormatException: Thrown when a method cannot parse an input string.
- o ArgumentNullException: Thrown when a method receives a null argument that it does not accept.
- o IndexOutOfRangeException: Thrown when attempting to access an element outside the bounds of an array or list.
- o NullReferenceException: Thrown when attempting to use a null object reference.

You can also create your own custom exception classes by inheriting from Exception.

5. **Throwing Exceptions** You can also explicitly throw exceptions using the throw keyword. This is useful when you want to signal an error in your own code.

Example:

csharp

```
if (number < 0)
{
    throw new ArgumentOutOfRangeException("Number cannot be negative");
}
```

Real-World Example: A Program That Handles Invalid User Input Gracefully

In this example, we will create a program that asks the user for their age and handles invalid input gracefully using try-catch blocks. If the user enters something other than a valid number, the program will catch the exception and display an error message instead of crashing.

Steps:

1. The program will ask the user to enter their age.
2. If the user enters a valid integer, the program will display the age.
3. If the user enters invalid input (non-numeric characters), the program will catch the exception and display an appropriate message.
4. The program will continue to prompt the user until valid input is provided.

Code:

```
csharp

using System;

class Program
{
    static void Main(string[] args)
    {
```

```csharp
        int age = 0;
        bool validInput = false;

        while (!validInput)
        {
          try
          {
            Console.Write("Please enter your age: ");
            age = int.Parse(Console.ReadLine());  // Try to parse the input as an integer
            validInput = true;  // If parsing is successful, exit the loop
          }
          catch (FormatException)
          {
            Console.WriteLine("Error: You must enter a valid number for age.");
          }
          catch (OverflowException)
          {
            Console.WriteLine("Error: The number entered is too large or too small.");
          }
        }

        Console.WriteLine($"Your age is: {age}");
      }
    }
```

Explanation:

- **Try Block**: The program attempts to parse the user input as an integer using int.Parse(). If the user enters a valid number, it assigns the value to the age variable and exits the loop.

- **Catch Blocks**:
  - **FormatException**: This exception is thrown if the user enters something that cannot be converted to an integer (e.g., text).

  - **OverflowException**: This exception is thrown if the user enters a number that is too large or too small to be stored in an int.

- **Valid Input Loop**: The program continues to ask the user for input until a valid number is entered.

Output Example:

yaml

Please enter your age: abc
Error: You must enter a valid number for age.
Please enter your age: -5000
Error: The number entered is too large or too small.
Please enter your age: 25
Your age is: 25

Real-World Use Case

Gracefully handling invalid user input is a common requirement in many applications, such as:

- **Forms and surveys**: Where you need to validate user input before submitting data.

- **Financial applications**: Ensuring that numerical input (e.g., amounts or percentages) is valid before performing calculations.

- **Data processing**: Ensuring that incoming data (such as CSV files or API responses) is correctly formatted and does not cause errors in the program.

By handling exceptions effectively, you can create programs that are more robust, user-friendly, and less likely to crash when faced with unexpected situations. This chapter introduces you to basic exception handling techniques that can be expanded to cover more complex error scenarios in real-world applications.

Chapter 11: Working with Files

Topics:

1. **Introduction to File I/O in C#** File I/O (Input/Output) operations allow your program to interact with the file system. In C#, the System.IO namespace provides classes and methods to read from and write to files, helping you persist data between program executions.

   Common File Operations:

   o **Reading from a file**: Retrieve data stored in a text file.

   o **Writing to a file**: Save or update data in a text file.

   o **Appending to a file**: Add data to the end of a file without overwriting existing data.

   o **Checking file existence**: Ensure that the file exists before performing operations.

   o **File paths**: Understanding how to specify file paths relative to your project or absolute paths.

2. **Reading from Files** You can read data from files in various ways. Some common methods include:

   o **File.ReadAllText()**: Reads the entire content of a file as a string.

- o **File.ReadAllLines()**: Reads the content of a file into an array, where each element represents a line from the file.

- o **StreamReader**: A more flexible way to read text from files line-by-line.

Example:

csharp

```
string content = File.ReadAllText("example.txt");
Console.WriteLine(content);
```

3. **Writing to Files** You can write data to files using several methods:

   - o **File.WriteAllText()**: Writes a string to a file, overwriting any existing content.

   - o **File.AppendAllText()**: Appends text to an existing file without overwriting the previous content.

   - o **StreamWriter**: Provides more flexibility for writing to files, including writing line-by-line.

Example:

csharp

```
string content = "Hello, world!";
File.WriteAllText("example.txt", content);
```

4. **Checking File Existence** Before reading from or writing to a file, it's a good practice to check whether the file exists. The File.Exists() method returns a Boolean indicating whether a specified file exists.

Example:

csharp

```
if (File.Exists("example.txt"))
{
    Console.WriteLine("File exists.");
}
else
{
    Console.WriteLine("File does not exist.");
}
```

5. **Working with File Paths**
   - o **Absolute Path**: Specifies the full path of the file, starting from the root directory (e.g., C:\Users\YourName\Documents\example.txt).
   - o **Relative Path**: Specifies the path relative to the program's current working directory (e.g., "example.txt").

Example (using relative path):

csharp

```
File.WriteAllText("data.txt", "Some content...");
```

Example (using absolute path):

csharp

```
File.WriteAllText(@"C:\Users\YourName\Documents\data.txt", "Some content...");
```

Real-World Example: A Program that Saves and Retrieves Data from a Text File

In this example, we will create a program that allows the user to save and retrieve a list of contacts from a text file. Each contact will consist of a name and phone number. The program will:

- Allow the user to add contacts to a text file.
- Display the list of contacts stored in the file.

Steps:

1. Create a text file (contacts.txt) to store contact information.
2. Implement functionality to add contacts to the file.
3. Implement functionality to read contacts from the file and display them.

Code:

csharp

```csharp
using System;
using System.IO;

class Program
{
    static string filePath = "contacts.txt";

    static void Main(string[] args)
    {
        // Display the menu to the user
        Console.WriteLine("Welcome to the Contact Management System");
        Console.WriteLine("1. Add a Contact");
        Console.WriteLine("2. Display Contacts");
        Console.WriteLine("3. Exit");

        bool continueRunning = true;

        while (continueRunning)
        {
            Console.Write("Choose an option (1-3): ");
            string choice = Console.ReadLine();

            switch (choice)
            {
                case "1":
                    AddContact();
                    break;
                case "2":
```

```
            DisplayContacts();
            break;
          case "3":
            continueRunning = false;
            Console.WriteLine("Goodbye!");
            break;
          default:
            Console.WriteLine("Invalid choice, please try again.");
            break;
        }
      }
}


// Method to add a new contact to the file
static void AddContact()
{
    Console.Write("Enter the contact's name: ");
    string name = Console.ReadLine();

    Console.Write("Enter the contact's phone number: ");
    string phone = Console.ReadLine();

    // Prepare the contact info as a string
    string contactInfo = $"{name}, {phone}";

    // Append the contact info to the file
    try
    {
        File.AppendAllText(filePath, contactInfo + Environment.NewLine);
        Console.WriteLine("Contact saved successfully!");
```

```csharp
        }
        catch (Exception ex)
        {
            Console.WriteLine($"Error: {ex.Message}");
        }
    }

    // Method to display all contacts from the file
    static void DisplayContacts()
    {
        if (File.Exists(filePath))
        {
            // Read all lines from the file and display them
            try
            {
                string[] contacts = File.ReadAllLines(filePath);
                if (contacts.Length == 0)
                {
                    Console.WriteLine("No contacts found.");
                }
                else
                {
                    Console.WriteLine("Contacts List:");
                    foreach (string contact in contacts)
                    {
                        Console.WriteLine(contact);
                    }
                }
            }
            catch (Exception ex)
```

```
    {
        Console.WriteLine($"Error: {ex.Message}");
    }
}
else
{
    Console.WriteLine("No contacts file found. Please add a contact first.");
}
  }
}
```

Explanation:

- **Adding a Contact**: The AddContact() method prompts the user for a name and phone number, then appends the information to the contacts.txt file using File.AppendAllText(). Each contact is saved on a new line.

- **Displaying Contacts**: The DisplayContacts() method checks if the file exists using File.Exists(). If it exists, the program reads all lines from the file using File.ReadAllLines(), then displays each contact.

- **Error Handling**: The program uses try-catch blocks to handle potential errors that may arise during file I/O operations, such as permissions issues or invalid paths.

Output Example:

vbnet

Welcome to the Contact Management System

1. Add a Contact

2. Display Contacts

3. Exit

Choose an option (1-3): 1

Enter the contact's name: John Doe

Enter the contact's phone number: 555-1234

Contact saved successfully!

Choose an option (1-3): 2

Contacts List:

John Doe, 555-1234

Real-World Use Case

This basic file I/O example can be extended to more complex applications, such as:

- **Personal Contact Management**: Where users can add, remove, and view their contacts.
- **Data Persistence**: Saving user preferences, settings, or logs between program executions.
- **Exporting and Importing Data**: For saving reports, exporting application data, or importing configuration files.

Mastering file I/O operations in C# is essential for applications that require data persistence, logging, or interacting with external data files. By understanding how to read from and write to files, you can enhance your applications with features like data storage and retrieval.

Chapter 12: Introduction to Windows Forms Applications

Topics:

1. **Overview of Windows Forms** Windows Forms is a UI (user interface) framework provided by Microsoft for building desktop applications that run on Windows. It allows developers to create graphical user interfaces (GUIs) with interactive components like buttons, text boxes, labels, and more.

   o **Event-Driven Programming**: Windows Forms is event-driven, meaning that the program responds to user interactions (events) such as clicks, key presses, and mouse movements.

   o **Controls**: Controls are the building blocks of Windows Forms applications. Examples include buttons, text boxes, labels, combo boxes, and more.

   o **Form**: A form is a window in a Windows Forms application. It acts as a container for controls and provides a structure for the user interface.

   o **Layout**: You can position controls on a form manually or use layout controls like panels and flow layouts to organize controls dynamically.

2. **Creating a Simple GUI Application** Creating a simple GUI application involves:

   o   Adding a Form to the project.

   o   Placing controls like buttons and labels on the form.

   o   Writing event handlers to respond to user actions.

Basic Components:

   o   **Form**: The main window of the application.

   o   **Button**: An interactive control that the user can click.

   o   **TextBox**: A control that allows the user to enter text.

   o   **Label**: A non-editable control used to display text.

Steps to Create a Windows Forms Application:

8.   **Create a Project**: In Visual Studio, create a new project and select "Windows Forms App" under the C# category.

   9.   **Design the Form**: Drag and drop controls onto the form using the Toolbox in Visual Studio.

   10. **Write Event Handlers**: Write code to handle events, such as button clicks, using event handlers.

3. **Event Handlers** An event handler is a method that responds to an event, such as a button click. Event handlers are connected to controls using the Click property, for example.

Example:

○ **Button Click Event**:

csharp

```
private void button1_Click(object sender, EventArgs e)
{
    MessageBox.Show("Button clicked!");
}
```

Real-World Example: A Basic Calculator Application with Buttons and Display

In this example, we will create a simple calculator application using Windows Forms. The calculator will have buttons for digits (0-9) and basic operations (addition, subtraction, multiplication, and division), as well as a display area to show the result.

Steps:

1. **Create a New Windows Forms Application**: In Visual Studio, create a new project and select "Windows Forms App (.NET Framework)" or "Windows Forms App (.NET Core)" depending on your setup.

2. **Design the Calculator Form**:
   ○ Add buttons for digits (0-9), operations (+, -, *, /), and other functions (C for clear, = for equals).

- o Add a TextBox control at the top to display the input and result.

3. **Write Event Handlers**: Implement event handlers to process button clicks and perform the necessary calculations.

Code:

csharp

```csharp
using System;
using System.Windows.Forms;

public partial class CalculatorForm : Form
{
    private double result = 0;
    private string operation = "";
    private bool isOperationClicked = false;

    public CalculatorForm()
    {
        InitializeComponent();
    }

    // Event handler for digit buttons
    private void Button_Click(object sender, EventArgs e)
    {
        if ((displayTextBox.Text == "0") || isOperationClicked)
        {
            displayTextBox.Clear();
        }
```

```csharp
    isOperationClicked = false;
    Button button = (Button)sender;
    displayTextBox.Text += button.Text;
}


// Event handler for the Clear button
private void ClearButton_Click(object sender, EventArgs e)
{
    displayTextBox.Text = "0";
    result = 0;
    operation = "";
}


// Event handler for the operation buttons
private void OperationButton_Click(object sender, EventArgs e)
{
    Button button = (Button)sender;
    operation = button.Text;
    result = Double.Parse(displayTextBox.Text);
    isOperationClicked = true;
}


// Event handler for the Equals button
private void EqualsButton_Click(object sender, EventArgs e)
{
    switch (operation)
    {
        case "+":
            displayTextBox.Text              =              (result              +
Double.Parse(displayTextBox.Text)).ToString();
```

```
        break;
    case "-":
        displayTextBox.Text          =          (result          -
Double.Parse(displayTextBox.Text)).ToString();
        break;
    case "*":
        displayTextBox.Text          =          (result          *
Double.Parse(displayTextBox.Text)).ToString();
        break;
    case "/":
        displayTextBox.Text          =          (result          /
Double.Parse(displayTextBox.Text)).ToString();
        break;
    }
    result = Double.Parse(displayTextBox.Text);
    operation = "";
  }
}
```

Explanation:

1. **Form Controls**:
   o A TextBox named displayTextBox is used to display the current input or result.
   o Multiple Button controls are added for digits (0-9), operations (+, -, *, /), and functions (C for clear, = for equals).

2. **Event Handlers**:

- o **Button_Click**: Handles digit button clicks. If the user clicks an operation button or the display is empty, it clears the TextBox.
- o **ClearButton_Click**: Clears the display and resets the result.
- o **OperationButton_Click**: Stores the current input in result and sets the operation to be performed (addition, subtraction, etc.).
- o **EqualsButton_Click**: Performs the calculation based on the selected operation and displays the result in the TextBox.

3. **Calculation Logic**:

- o The EqualsButton_Click method checks the selected operation and performs the corresponding mathematical operation on the current result and input, updating the TextBox with the result.

Form Design (UI Elements):

- A TextBox (named displayTextBox) to display the current input and result.
- Buttons for digits (0-9), operations (+, -, *, /), clear (C), and equals (=).

Real-World Use Case

This basic calculator application is a great starting point for creating more complex Windows Forms applications. You could expand this program to include more advanced features, such as:

- **Memory functions**: Adding memory buttons (e.g., M+, M-, MR for storing and recalling values).
- **Scientific calculator**: Adding trigonometric functions, square roots, and logarithms.
- **History**: Displaying a history of calculations.

Windows Forms is widely used for creating desktop applications in industries ranging from finance and accounting to education and healthcare. By mastering the basics of Windows Forms, you can build interactive, user-friendly desktop applications that run on Windows systems.

Chapter 13: Event Handling in Windows Forms

Topics:

1. **Understanding Events and Event Handlers** Events are actions or occurrences that happen in an application, such as user interactions (clicks, key presses), system-generated events, or timers. Event handlers are methods that are triggered in response to these events. In Windows Forms applications, events are usually generated by user actions, such as clicking a button, typing in a text box, or changing a control's value.

   o **Event**: An event represents an action or occurrence that can be handled by the program.

   o **Event Handler**: An event handler is a method that contains the code to execute when an event is raised.

Basic Event Handling Process:

3.   **Define an event**: An event is usually defined by controls such as buttons or textboxes in Windows Forms applications.

   4. **Create an event handler**: An event handler is a method that is bound to an event and defines the actions to take when the event occurs.

5. **Wire the event to the handler**: In Visual Studio, this is done automatically when you double-click a control or manually attach the event handler to an event in code.

2. **Common Events in Windows Forms** Common events in Windows Forms include:

   o **Click**: Triggered when a button is clicked.

   o **TextChanged**: Triggered when the text of a TextBox is changed.

   o **MouseEnter**: Triggered when the mouse pointer enters the bounds of a control.

   o **KeyDown**: Triggered when a key is pressed down while the control has focus.

Example:

csharp

```
button1.Click += new EventHandler(Button1_Click);
```

This attaches the Button1_Click event handler to the Click event of button1.

3. **Event Handler Syntax** Event handler methods follow a specific signature, where the first parameter is usually the sender (the object raising the event), and the second parameter contains event-specific data.

Example:

csharp

```
private void Button1_Click(object sender, EventArgs e)
{
    // Code to handle the click event
}
```

- o   sender: The object that raised the event (in this case, button1).
- o   e: EventArgs contains event data (if applicable).

4. **Handling User Input** Handling user input is one of the most common scenarios for event handling in a Windows Forms application. Input can be captured from various controls like buttons, textboxes, and other interactive elements.

   Example: Handling button click events to change the text of a label.

Real-World Example: A Program That Tracks Button Clicks and Updates the Display Accordingly

In this example, we will create a simple program that tracks the number of times a button is clicked and updates a label to display the current count.

Steps:

1. Create a button that the user can click.
2. Create a label to display the number of clicks.
3. Create an event handler for the button's Click event to update the label each time the button is clicked.

Code:

csharp

```csharp
using System;
using System.Windows.Forms;

public partial class ClickCounterForm : Form
{
    // Initialize click count
    private int clickCount = 0;

    public ClickCounterForm()
    {
        InitializeComponent();
    }

    // Event handler for button click
    private void ButtonClickHandler(object sender, EventArgs e)
    {
        // Increment click count
        clickCount++;
```

```csharp
            // Update the label to display the current click count
            clickLabel.Text = "Button clicked: " + clickCount.ToString() + " times";
    }


    // Form components (auto-generated by Visual Studio)
    private Button clickButton;
    private Label clickLabel;

    private void InitializeComponent()
    {
        this.clickButton = new Button();
        this.clickLabel = new Label();

        //
        // clickButton
        //
        this.clickButton.Location = new System.Drawing.Point(100, 100);
        this.clickButton.Name = "clickButton";
        this.clickButton.Size = new System.Drawing.Size(120, 40);
        this.clickButton.Text = "Click Me!";
        this.clickButton.Click                        +=                    new
System.EventHandler(this.ButtonClickHandler);


        //
        // clickLabel
        //
        this.clickLabel.Location = new System.Drawing.Point(100, 160);
        this.clickLabel.Name = "clickLabel";
        this.clickLabel.Size = new System.Drawing.Size(200, 30);
        this.clickLabel.Text = "Button clicked: 0 times";
```

```
//
// ClickCounterForm
//
this.ClientSize = new System.Drawing.Size(400, 300);
this.Controls.Add(this.clickButton);
this.Controls.Add(this.clickLabel);
this.Name = "ClickCounterForm";
this.Text = "Button Click Tracker";
    }
}
```

Explanation:

1. **Form Design**:
   - We have a Button named clickButton and a Label named clickLabel.
   - The button is positioned at (100, 100), and the label is positioned below the button at (100, 160).

2. **Event Handler**:
   - The event handler ButtonClickHandler is attached to the Click event of the button.
   - Each time the button is clicked, the clickCount is incremented, and the label text is updated to display the current number of clicks.

3. **Label Update**:

- o The label's text is updated using the clickLabel.Text property. We use clickCount.ToString() to convert the integer into a string for display.

4. **Form Components**:
   - o The components (clickButton and clickLabel) are defined and initialized in the InitializeComponent method, which is automatically generated by Visual Studio when you design the form in the Visual Studio designer.

Output Example:

When you run the application, the window will show:

- A button labeled **"Click Me!"**.
- A label showing **"Button clicked: 0 times"** initially.

Each time the user clicks the button, the label will update:

bash

```
Button clicked: 1 times
Button clicked: 2 times
Button clicked: 3 times
```

Real-World Use Case

This event handling example of a button click counter can be expanded into various practical applications:

- **Quiz Applications**: Track the number of correct answers a user selects and display feedback.
- **Form Validation**: Trigger validation checks when the user interacts with form controls.
- **Data Entry**: Automatically update fields when the user clicks buttons or interacts with dropdowns and checkboxes.
- **Games**: Track user interactions, such as button clicks, to simulate actions like scorekeeping or game progress.

By understanding event handling in Windows Forms, you can build interactive applications that respond to user actions in a way that enhances the user experience. This knowledge is essential for creating robust, responsive desktop applications.

Chapter 14: Controls in Windows Forms

Topics:

1. **Working with Buttons** Buttons are one of the most commonly used controls in Windows Forms applications. A button control can trigger actions when clicked by the user.

   - **Basic Usage**: To create a button, drag it from the Toolbox onto the form or create it programmatically. Buttons have properties like Text (the label on the button) and Size.

   - **Event Handling**: The most common event for buttons is the Click event. You can attach an event handler to perform actions when the user clicks the button.

   Example:

   csharp

```
Button myButton = new Button();
myButton.Text = "Click Me!";
myButton.Click += new EventHandler(MyButton_Click);

private void MyButton_Click(object sender, EventArgs e)
{
    MessageBox.Show("Button was clicked!");
}
```

2. **Working with Labels** Labels are used to display static text on a form. Labels cannot be edited by the user, and their text can be changed programmatically.

   o **Basic Usage**: To create a label, drag it from the Toolbox or create it programmatically. You can set the Text property to display messages.

   o **Common Properties**:

     ▪ Text: The text displayed on the label.

     ▪ Font: Defines the font used to display the text.

     ▪ AutoSize: If set to true, the label automatically adjusts its size to fit the text.

Example:

csharp

```
Label myLabel = new Label();
myLabel.Text = "Enter your name:";
myLabel.Location = new Point(10, 10);
myLabel.Size = new Size(200, 20);
```

3. **Working with TextBoxes** TextBoxes are used for user input. They allow the user to enter text, such as their name, email, or address.

   o **Basic Usage**: To create a TextBox, drag it from the Toolbox or create it programmatically. You can set properties such as Text (the default value of the

TextBox), Multiline (for multi-line input), and PasswordChar (for password inputs).

- o **Common Properties**:
  - Text: The current text entered in the TextBox.
  - Multiline: If true, the TextBox supports multiple lines of text.
  - MaxLength: The maximum number of characters the user can type into the TextBox.

Example:

csharp

```
TextBox myTextBox = new TextBox();
myTextBox.Text = "";
myTextBox.Location = new Point(10, 40);
myTextBox.Size = new Size(200, 20);
```

4. **Other Common Controls**

- o **ComboBox**: A drop-down list that allows users to select from predefined options.
- o **CheckBox**: Allows users to make a binary choice (checked or unchecked).
- o **RadioButton**: Used for selecting one option from a set of predefined options.
- o **GroupBox**: Used to group related controls together.

Real-World Example: Creating a Form to Gather User Information (e.g., Name and Email)

In this example, we will create a Windows Forms application where the user can enter their name and email. The form will include:

- TextBoxes for the user to input their name and email.
- Labels to guide the user on what information to enter.
- A Button to submit the information.

Steps:

1. Add labels to indicate what data the user needs to provide.
2. Add TextBoxes for the user to input their name and email.
3. Add a Button to submit the information.
4. Handle the Button's Click event to display a message with the entered information.

Code:

csharp

```csharp
using System;
using System.Windows.Forms;

public partial class UserInfoForm : Form
{
    // Constructor for initializing the form
    public UserInfoForm()
```

```csharp
{
    InitializeComponent();
}

// Event handler for the submit button
private void SubmitButton_Click(object sender, EventArgs e)
{
    string name = nameTextBox.Text;  // Get text from nameTextBox
    string email = emailTextBox.Text;  // Get text from emailTextBox

    // Display user information
    MessageBox.Show($"Name:       {name}\nEmail:       {email}",       "User
Information");
}

// Form components (auto-generated by Visual Studio)
private Label nameLabel;
private Label emailLabel;
private TextBox nameTextBox;
private TextBox emailTextBox;
private Button submitButton;

// Method to initialize the form's components
private void InitializeComponent()
{
    // Initialize controls
    this.nameLabel = new Label();
    this.emailLabel = new Label();
    this.nameTextBox = new TextBox();
    this.emailTextBox = new TextBox();
```

```
this.submitButton = new Button();

//
// nameLabel
//
this.nameLabel.Text = "Enter your name:";
this.nameLabel.Location = new Point(10, 10);
this.nameLabel.Size = new Size(200, 20);

//
// emailLabel
//
this.emailLabel.Text = "Enter your email:";
this.emailLabel.Location = new Point(10, 40);
this.emailLabel.Size = new Size(200, 20);

//
// nameTextBox
//
this.nameTextBox.Location = new Point(10, 30);
this.nameTextBox.Size = new Size(200, 20);

//
// emailTextBox
//
this.emailTextBox.Location = new Point(10, 60);
this.emailTextBox.Size = new Size(200, 20);

//
// submitButton
```

```csharp
//
this.submitButton.Text = "Submit";
this.submitButton.Location = new Point(10, 90);
this.submitButton.Size = new Size(100, 30);
this.submitButton.Click += new EventHandler(SubmitButton_Click);


//
// UserInfoForm
//
this.ClientSize = new Size(300, 150);
this.Controls.Add(this.nameLabel);
this.Controls.Add(this.emailLabel);
this.Controls.Add(this.nameTextBox);
this.Controls.Add(this.emailTextBox);
this.Controls.Add(this.submitButton);
this.Text = "User Information Form";
    }
}
```

Explanation:

1. **Form Components**:
   - **Labels** (nameLabel and emailLabel) are used to prompt the user for their name and email.
   - **TextBoxes** (nameTextBox and emailTextBox) allow the user to enter their name and email.
   - **Button** (submitButton) is used to submit the entered information.

2. **Event Handling**:

- o The SubmitButton_Click event handler is triggered when the user clicks the submit button.
- o The handler retrieves the entered name and email from the TextBox controls and displays a message box with the user's information.

3. **Layout**:

- o The controls are positioned using the Location property.
- o The form is sized using ClientSize to ensure all controls fit within the form.

Output Example:

When you run the application:

1. The user will see two fields (name and email) and a submit button.
2. After entering their name and email and clicking **Submit**, a message box will appear with the following information:

makefile

Name: John Doe
Email: john.doe@example.com

Real-World Use Case

This form can be extended and used in several real-world applications, such as:

- **User Registration Forms**: Collecting basic information (e.g., name, email, password).
- **Contact Forms**: Collecting user inquiries or feedback, with additional fields for message or subject.
- **Survey Forms**: Gathering answers to specific questions and storing or processing the responses.

By mastering Windows Forms controls like buttons, labels, and text boxes, you can create rich, interactive desktop applications with user-friendly interfaces for a variety of purposes.

Chapter 15: Advanced Data Handling in C#

Topics:

1. **Working with Arrays** Arrays are used to store multiple values in a single variable. In C#, arrays are fixed in size, which means the number of elements in an array cannot be changed after the array is created. They are useful when you know in advance the number of items you need to store.

   o **Declaring and Initializing Arrays**:

   csharp

   ```csharp
   int[] numbers = new int[5]; // Array of integers with 5 elements
   numbers[0] = 10; // Assigning values to array elements
   ```

   You can also initialize an array at the time of declaration:

   csharp

   ```csharp
   int[] numbers = { 10, 20, 30, 40, 50 };
   ```

   o **Accessing Array Elements**:

   csharp

   ```csharp
   int firstNumber = numbers[0]; // Accessing the first element
   ```

2. **Working with Lists** A List<T> is a generic collection that can grow and shrink dynamically, unlike arrays. Lists are ideal when the size of the collection is unknown or can change.

   o **Creating a List**:

   csharp

   ```
   List<int> numbers = new List<int>();
   numbers.Add(10); // Adding elements to the list
   numbers.Add(20);
   ```

   o **Accessing List Elements**:

   csharp

   ```
   int firstNumber = numbers[0]; // Accessing the first element
   ```

   o **Removing Elements**:

   csharp

   ```
   numbers.Remove(10); // Removes the first occurrence of 10
   ```

3. **Working with Dictionaries** A Dictionary<TKey, TValue> is a collection of key-value pairs. Dictionaries are useful when you need to store and retrieve data based on a unique key.

   o **Creating a Dictionary**:

csharp

```csharp
Dictionary<int, string> contacts = new Dictionary<int, string>();
contacts.Add(1, "John Doe");  // Adding key-value pairs to the dictionary
contacts.Add(2, "Jane Smith");
```

- o **Accessing Dictionary Elements**:

csharp

```csharp
string contactName = contacts[1];  // Accessing a value using the key
```

- o **Removing Elements**:

csharp

```csharp
contacts.Remove(1);  // Removes the item with key 1
```

4. **Other Advanced Data Structures** C# offers several advanced data structures that are useful in specific scenarios:
   - o **Queue**: A FIFO (first-in, first-out) collection.
   - o **Stack**: A LIFO (last-in, first-out) collection.
   - o **HashSet**: A collection that stores unique values and performs fast lookups.

Example of a Queue:

csharp

```
Queue<string> queue = new Queue<string>();
queue.Enqueue("Task 1");  // Adds an item to the queue
queue.Enqueue("Task 2");

string task = queue.Dequeue();  // Removes and returns the first item
```

Real-World Example: Building a Contact Manager Application Using Lists and Dictionaries

In this example, we will build a simple contact manager application using a **List** and a **Dictionary** to manage contacts. The user will be able to add contacts, display contacts, and search for a contact by their ID. The contacts will be stored in a **Dictionary** for fast access by ID and in a **List** for displaying all contacts.

Steps:

1. Use a Dictionary<int, string> to store contacts where the key is the contact ID and the value is the contact's name.
2. Provide functionality to add, display, and search contacts.
3. Display the contacts in a list format for the user.

Code:

csharp

```csharp
using System;
using System.Collections.Generic;

public class ContactManager
{
    // Dictionary to store contacts, where key is the contact ID and value is the
contact name
    private Dictionary<int, string> contacts = new Dictionary<int, string>();

    // Method to add a new contact
    public void AddContact(int id, string name)
    {
        if (!contacts.ContainsKey(id))
        {
            contacts.Add(id, name);
            Console.WriteLine($"Contact added: {id} - {name}");
        }
        else
        {
            Console.WriteLine("A contact with this ID already exists.");
        }
    }

    // Method to display all contacts
    public void DisplayContacts()
    {
        if (contacts.Count == 0)
        {
            Console.WriteLine("No contacts available.");
        }
```

```csharp
        else
        {
            Console.WriteLine("Contacts List:");
            foreach (var contact in contacts)
            {
                Console.WriteLine($"ID: {contact.Key}, Name: {contact.Value}");
            }
        }
    }

    // Method to search for a contact by ID
    public void SearchContact(int id)
    {
        if (contacts.ContainsKey(id))
        {
            Console.WriteLine($"Found contact: {id} - {contacts[id]}");
        }
        else
        {
            Console.WriteLine("Contact not found.");
        }
    }
}

class Program
{
    static void Main(string[] args)
    {
        ContactManager manager = new ContactManager();
```

```
// Adding some contacts
manager.AddContact(1, "John Doe");
manager.AddContact(2, "Jane Smith");
manager.AddContact(3, "Alice Johnson");

// Displaying all contacts
manager.DisplayContacts();

// Searching for a specific contact by ID
Console.WriteLine("\nSearching for contact with ID 2:");
manager.SearchContact(2);

Console.WriteLine("\nSearching for contact with ID 5:");
manager.SearchContact(5);
    }
}
```

Explanation:

1. **Dictionary for Storing Contacts**:
   o We use a Dictionary<int, string> where the key is the contact ID (an integer) and the value is the contact's name (a string).
   o The AddContact method checks if the ID already exists in the dictionary and adds the contact only if the ID is unique.

2. **Displaying All Contacts**:
   o The DisplayContacts method iterates over the dictionary and displays all contacts by printing the

key-value pairs. The contacts are displayed in the format: ID: 1, Name: John Doe.

3. **Searching for Contacts**:

   o The SearchContact method takes an ID and searches for it in the dictionary. If the ID exists, it prints the contact name; otherwise, it displays "Contact not found."

Output Example:

yaml

Contact added: 1 - John Doe

Contact added: 2 - Jane Smith

Contact added: 3 - Alice Johnson

Contacts List:

ID: 1, Name: John Doe

ID: 2, Name: Jane Smith

ID: 3, Name: Alice Johnson

Searching for contact with ID 2:

Found contact: 2 - Jane Smith

Searching for contact with ID 5:

Contact not found.

Real-World Use Case

This contact manager example can be expanded into a full-fledged application, such as:

- **Personal or Business Contact Management Systems**: Storing, searching, and managing a list of contacts for personal or business use.
- **CRM (Customer Relationship Management) Systems**: Storing customer information, tracking interactions, and managing communication history.
- **Data Entry Systems**: For entering, updating, and searching large sets of data, such as employee records or inventory management.

By mastering advanced data handling with collections like Lists and Dictionaries, you can create efficient, scalable applications that manage and process large amounts of data.

Chapter 16: Debugging Your Code

Topics:

1. **Techniques for Debugging in Visual Studio** Debugging is a critical part of the software development process, allowing you to find and fix errors in your code. Visual Studio provides several powerful tools for debugging, which help identify issues, inspect values, and understand the flow of the application during runtime.

   Common Debugging Techniques:

   o **Breakpoints**: A breakpoint pauses the program's execution at a specific point, allowing you to inspect the values of variables and step through the code.

   o **Step-Through Debugging**: This allows you to execute the program line by line, making it easier to see where things go wrong.

   o **Watch Window**: You can watch the values of variables as the program runs, which helps track down where a value may be incorrect.

   o **Immediate Window**: You can execute code or check variable values while the program is paused at a breakpoint.

- o **Call Stack**: The call stack window shows you the order of method calls that led to the current point in the program.

2. **Using Breakpoints** A breakpoint is a marker that you can set on a line of code. When the program reaches this line, execution will pause, allowing you to inspect variable values, call stack, and step through the code.

Setting a Breakpoint:

- o To set a breakpoint, click in the left margin of the code window, next to the line number, or press F9 while on the line you want to break at.
- o When a breakpoint is hit, the program will pause, and you can inspect the state of the application.

Using the Debug Toolbar:

- o **Continue (F5)**: Resumes the program's execution until the next breakpoint or the end.
- o **Step Over (F10)**: Executes the current line of code and moves to the next line.
- o **Step Into (F11)**: Steps into a method call to debug inside that method.
- o **Step Out (Shift + F11)**: Steps out of the current method and goes back to the caller method.

3. **Step-Through Debugging** Step-through debugging allows you to observe the execution of your program step-by-step, which is especially useful for finding logical errors or unexpected behavior.

   o **Step Over**: Use F10 to step over method calls without diving into them.

   o **Step Into**: Use F11 to go inside a method call and inspect its behavior.

   o **Step Out**: Use Shift + F11 to quickly exit a method and go back to the caller.

4. **Watch and Immediate Windows**

   o **Watch Window**: You can add variables or expressions to the Watch window to monitor their values during runtime.

   o **Immediate Window**: Allows you to run commands or evaluate expressions during a debugging session.

Example:

   o To evaluate an expression in the Immediate window, type myVariable and press Enter to see its value.

Real-World Example: Debugging a Simple Bug in a Windows Forms Application

In this example, we will create a basic Windows Forms application with a bug, and we'll debug it step-by-step to fix the issue. The application will have a button and a label, and when the button is clicked, the label will display the current count. However, there's a bug: the counter isn't increasing as expected.

Steps:

1. **Create a New Windows Forms Application**: The form will have a button and a label. The button will increment a counter and display it on the label.
2. **Introduce a Bug**: We'll introduce an issue where the counter doesn't update as expected.
3. **Debug the Bug**: We'll use breakpoints, step-through debugging, and the Watch window to fix the issue.

Code with Bug:

csharp

```csharp
using System;
using System.Windows.Forms;

public partial class CounterForm : Form
{
    private int count = 0;

    public CounterForm()
    {
```

```
    InitializeComponent();
}

private void incrementButton_Click(object sender, EventArgs e)
{
    // Bug: The count is being reset to 0 every time the button is clicked
    count = 0;  // This line should not reset the counter to 0
    countLabel.Text = "Count: " + count.ToString();
}
}
```

Steps to Debug:

1. **Set a Breakpoint**:
   - Set a breakpoint at the incrementButton_Click method (on the line where count is assigned 0).

2. **Run the Application**:
   - Start the application by pressing F5 (or clicking on the Start button in Visual Studio).
   - Click the **Increment** button.

3. **Hit the Breakpoint**:
   - The program will pause at the breakpoint in the incrementButton_Click method.
   - You can now inspect the value of count using the **Watch window**. Initially, it's 0, but when you step through the code, it gets reset to 0 every time the button is clicked.

4. **Step Through the Code**:

- o Press F10 (Step Over) to move through the code line-by-line.
- o Notice that the count = 0 line resets the counter to 0 each time.

5. **Inspect and Fix the Bug**:
   - o The bug is that count is being reset to 0 every time the button is clicked, rather than incrementing it. To fix this, we need to remove the count = 0 line and change the code to increment count by 1.

Fixed Code:

csharp

```
private void incrementButton_Click(object sender, EventArgs e)
{
    // Corrected: Increment the count instead of resetting it
    count++; // This increments the counter by 1
    countLabel.Text = "Count: " + count.ToString();
}
```

6. **Test the Fixed Application**:
   - o Run the application again. Now, each time you click the button, the counter will increment correctly, and the label will update accordingly.

Output Example:
Before fixing the bug:

makefile

Count: 0
(Click button multiple times)
Count: 0

After fixing the bug:

makefile

Count: 1
(Click button multiple times)
Count: 2
Count: 3

Real-World Use Case

This debugging example can be expanded to more complex applications where:

- **User Input Validation**: You debug forms where the data entered by users needs to be validated before submitting.
- **Calculations and Logic Errors**: Debugging issues related to the incorrect calculation or logic errors in business rules.
- **UI Issues**: Debugging unexpected UI behavior, such as controls not displaying the correct data or not updating when expected.

Visual Studio's debugging tools, such as breakpoints, step-through debugging, and the Watch window, are essential for efficiently finding and fixing issues in your code, making the development process much smoother and more productive. Debugging skills are essential for creating reliable applications and ensuring they work as expected in a variety of scenarios.

Chapter 17: Introduction to LINQ (Language Integrated Query)

Topics:

1. **What is LINQ?** LINQ (Language Integrated Query) is a powerful feature in C# that allows you to query and manipulate collections of data (like arrays, lists, and databases) directly in C# using a syntax that is integrated into the language. LINQ simplifies data queries and manipulations by allowing developers to write SQL-like queries using C# syntax, making data handling much more intuitive.

   Key Benefits of LINQ:

   o **Concise Syntax**: LINQ provides a compact and readable syntax for querying and manipulating data.

   o **Type Safety**: LINQ queries are strongly typed, meaning the compiler can catch errors at compile time.

   o **Support for Multiple Data Sources**: LINQ can be used with various data sources, including arrays, lists, databases, XML, and more.

2. **LINQ Query Syntax vs. Method Syntax** LINQ can be used with two types of syntax:

- **Query Syntax**: Similar to SQL and looks more declarative.
- **Method Syntax**: Uses methods like Where(), OrderBy(), Select(), etc., to build queries in a more functional style.

Query Syntax Example:

csharp

```
var result = from c in contacts
        where c.Age > 30
        orderby c.Name
        select c;
```

Method Syntax Example:

csharp

```
var result = contacts.Where(c => c.Age > 30)
        .OrderBy(c => c.Name)
        .Select(c => c);
```

3. **Common LINQ Operators**

- **Where()**: Filters data based on a condition.
- **OrderBy()**: Sorts data in ascending order.
- **OrderByDescending()**: Sorts data in descending order.
- **Select()**: Projects each element of a collection into a new form.

- o **GroupBy()**: Groups data based on a key.
- o **First()**: Returns the first element that matches the condition.
- o **ToList()**: Converts the result into a list.
- o **Count()**: Counts the number of elements in a collection.

4. **Deferred Execution vs. Immediate Execution**

- o **Deferred Execution**: LINQ queries are not executed immediately. Instead, they are executed when the query is iterated over (e.g., with foreach).
- o **Immediate Execution**: Methods like ToList(), ToArray(), Count(), and First() cause immediate execution, meaning the query is executed right away.

5. **Using LINQ with Collections** LINQ can be used with various in-memory collections, including arrays, lists, dictionaries, etc.

Example:

csharp

```
List<int> numbers = new List<int> { 1, 2, 3, 4, 5 };
var evenNumbers = numbers.Where(n => n % 2 == 0).ToList();
```

Real-World Example: Writing a LINQ Query to Filter and Sort a List of Contacts

In this example, we will build a contact manager application that uses LINQ to filter and sort a list of contacts. Each contact will have a name, age, and email. We will write a LINQ query to:

- Filter contacts that are over 30 years old.
- Sort them alphabetically by name.

Steps:

1. Create a class Contact with properties like Name, Age, and Email.
2. Create a list of Contact objects.
3. Write a LINQ query to filter and sort the list.
4. Display the results in the console.

Code:

csharp

```csharp
using System;
using System.Collections.Generic;
using System.Linq;

public class Contact
{
    public string Name { get; set; }
    public int Age { get; set; }
    public string Email { get; set; }
```

```csharp
    public Contact(string name, int age, string email)
    {
        Name = name;
        Age = age;
        Email = email;
    }
}

class Program
{
    static void Main(string[] args)
    {
        // Creating a list of contacts
        List<Contact> contacts = new List<Contact>
        {
            new Contact("John Doe", 28, "john@example.com"),
            new Contact("Jane Smith", 35, "jane@example.com"),
            new Contact("Alice Johnson", 42, "alice@example.com"),
            new Contact("Bob Brown", 30, "bob@example.com")
        };

        // LINQ query to filter contacts over 30 years old and sort by name
        var filteredContacts = from c in contacts
                    where c.Age > 30
                    orderby c.Name
                    select c;

        // Display the filtered and sorted contacts
        Console.WriteLine("Contacts over 30, sorted by name:");
        foreach (var contact in filteredContacts)
```

```
    {
        Console.WriteLine($"{contact.Name},    Age:    {contact.Age},    Email:
{contact.Email}");
    }


    // Alternatively, using method syntax:
    Console.WriteLine("\nMethod Syntax - Contacts over 30, sorted by name:");
    var filteredContactsMethodSyntax = contacts.Where(c => c.Age > 30)
                        .OrderBy(c => c.Name);

    foreach (var contact in filteredContactsMethodSyntax)
    {
        Console.WriteLine($"{contact.Name},    Age:    {contact.Age},    Email:
{contact.Email}");
    }
  }
}
```

Explanation:

1. **Contact Class**: A simple class with three properties: Name, Age, and Email. The constructor initializes these properties.
2. **List of Contacts**: A list of Contact objects is created with different values for name, age, and email.
3. **LINQ Query**:
   - **Query Syntax**: The LINQ query filters contacts older than 30 years and orders them alphabetically by their name.

o **Method Syntax**: The same query is written using method syntax with Where() for filtering and OrderBy() for sorting.

4. **Displaying Results**: The filtered and sorted contacts are displayed using a foreach loop.

Output Example:

yaml

Contacts over 30, sorted by name:
Alice Johnson, Age: 42, Email: alice@example.com
Jane Smith, Age: 35, Email: jane@example.com

Method Syntax - Contacts over 30, sorted by name:
Alice Johnson, Age: 42, Email: alice@example.com
Jane Smith, Age: 35, Email: jane@example.com

Real-World Use Case

This LINQ query example can be applied to many real-world scenarios:

- **Filtering and Sorting Customer Lists**: A contact manager or CRM system could filter customers by age or last purchase date and sort them based on their names or locations.

- **Employee Data**: Filtering employees based on their departments or years of service, and sorting them by name or salary.

- **Inventory Management**: Filtering products by category or price range, and sorting them by name or stock quantity.

LINQ simplifies querying and manipulating data collections, making it a powerful tool for developers when working with in-memory data. By understanding and applying LINQ, you can write more concise, readable, and maintainable code when working with collections in C#.

Chapter 18: Understanding Inheritance and Polymorphism

Topics:

1. **What is Inheritance?** Inheritance is a fundamental concept in object-oriented programming (OOP) that allows one class (called the **child class** or **derived class**) to inherit properties and methods from another class (called the **base class** or **parent class**). Inheritance allows for code reuse, and it helps you model hierarchical relationships between objects.

   Key Benefits of Inheritance:

   o **Code Reusability**: A derived class can use the code in its base class, reducing redundancy.

   o **Extensibility**: You can extend or modify the behavior of a base class in derived classes.

   o **Maintainability**: Changes made to the base class automatically propagate to the derived classes.

2. **Creating Child Classes (Derived Classes)** A derived class is created by using the : base keyword. It can access all public and protected members of the base class, but it can also define its own unique members or override base class methods.

Example:

csharp

```csharp
class Vehicle
{
    public string Make { get; set; }
    public string Model { get; set; }

    public void StartEngine()
    {
        Console.WriteLine("Starting engine...");
    }
}

class Car : Vehicle  // Car is a derived class of Vehicle
{
    public int Doors { get; set; }

    // Additional functionality or overrides can be added here
}
```

3. **Overriding Methods** In C#, derived classes can **override** methods of the base class. This is done using the override keyword. Overriding allows a derived class to provide its own implementation of a method that was already defined in the base class.

Example:

csharp

```csharp
class Vehicle
{
    public virtual void StartEngine()
    {
        Console.WriteLine("Starting vehicle engine...");
    }
}

class Car : Vehicle
{
    public override void StartEngine() // Overriding the base class method
    {
        Console.WriteLine("Starting car engine...");
    }
}
```

In this example, the Car class overrides the StartEngine method, providing a specific implementation for cars.

4. **What is Polymorphism?** Polymorphism allows objects of different classes to be treated as objects of a common base class. The most common way to achieve polymorphism in C# is through method overriding.

   Two Types of Polymorphism:

- o **Compile-time polymorphism (Method Overloading)**: Methods with the same name but different signatures.
- o **Runtime polymorphism (Method Overriding)**: The method that gets executed is determined at runtime based on the object's actual type.

Example:

csharp

Vehicle vehicle = new Car(); // Polymorphism: Car is treated as Vehicle
vehicle.StartEngine();   // Outputs: "Starting car engine..."

In this example, even though the reference variable vehicle is of type Vehicle, it points to an object of type Car. When the StartEngine method is called, the overridden method in Car is invoked.

5. **The virtual and override Keywords**
   - o **virtual**: The method in the base class that can be overridden by derived classes.
   - o **override**: The method in the derived class that provides its own implementation of a base class method.

Real-World Example: A Program with a Base Class "Vehicle" and Derived Classes "Car" and "Truck"

In this example, we will create a base class Vehicle with derived classes Car and Truck. We will use inheritance to reuse code, override methods to provide specific behavior for each type of vehicle, and demonstrate polymorphism.

Steps:

1. Define a base class Vehicle with common properties and methods.
2. Create derived classes Car and Truck, each overriding a method to provide specific behavior.
3. Demonstrate polymorphism by creating a Vehicle reference and assigning it both Car and Truck objects.

Code:

csharp

```csharp
using System;

public class Vehicle
{
    public string Make { get; set; }
    public string Model { get; set; }

    public virtual void StartEngine()
```

```csharp
        {
            Console.WriteLine("Starting the engine...");
        }

        public void StopEngine()
        {
            Console.WriteLine("Stopping the engine...");
        }
    }

public class Car : Vehicle
{
        public int Doors { get; set; }

        public override void StartEngine()
        {
            Console.WriteLine("Starting the car engine...");
        }
    }

public class Truck : Vehicle
{
        public int LoadCapacity { get; set; }

        public override void StartEngine()
        {
            Console.WriteLine("Starting the truck engine...");
        }
    }
```

```
class Program
{
    static void Main()
    {
        // Polymorphism: Creating a Vehicle reference but assigning Car and Truck objects
        Vehicle myCar = new Car { Make = "Toyota", Model = "Corolla", Doors = 4 };
        Vehicle myTruck = new Truck { Make = "Ford", Model = "F-150", LoadCapacity = 1000 };

        // Demonstrating polymorphism by calling the StartEngine method
        myCar.StartEngine();   // Outputs: "Starting the car engine..."
        myTruck.StartEngine(); // Outputs: "Starting the truck engine..."

        // Using common methods from the base class
        myCar.StopEngine();    // Outputs: "Stopping the engine..."
        myTruck.StopEngine();  // Outputs: "Stopping the engine..."
    }
}
```

Explanation:

1. **Base Class Vehicle:**
   - Vehicle contains common properties like Make and Model, and methods like StartEngine and StopEngine.
   - The StartEngine method is marked as virtual to allow derived classes to override it.

2. **Derived Classes Car and Truck:**

- o Car and Truck both inherit from Vehicle and override the StartEngine method to provide their own specific implementation.
- o The Car class has a property Doors, and the Truck class has a property LoadCapacity, both of which are unique to their respective classes.

3. **Polymorphism**:

- o In the Main method, myCar and myTruck are references of type Vehicle, but they point to objects of type Car and Truck, respectively.
- o The StartEngine method is overridden in both derived classes. When StartEngine is called on myCar and myTruck, the correct method (from Car or Truck) is executed, demonstrating runtime polymorphism.

Output:

Starting the car engine...
Starting the truck engine...
Stopping the engine...
Stopping the engine...

Real-World Use Case

This example of inheritance and polymorphism can be applied in various real-world scenarios:

- **Vehicle Management Systems**: Where you can have different types of vehicles (cars, trucks, motorcycles) and manage their specific behaviors, such as starting the engine, stopping the engine, and loading cargo.

- **Employee Management**: A base Employee class could be extended by classes like Manager, Developer, and Salesperson, each overriding methods such as CalculateSalary based on specific rules for each type.

- **Game Development**: In games, you could have a base Character class with derived classes like Warrior, Mage, and Archer, where each character has different abilities and stats.

Understanding inheritance and polymorphism is essential for creating flexible and reusable code, allowing for easier maintenance and extension of applications. This knowledge is foundational for object-oriented design and is widely used in many software engineering disciplines.

Chapter 19: Working with Databases in C#

Topics:

1. **Introduction to Databases A database** is a structured collection of data that can be accessed and manipulated by software applications. Databases are used to store and organize data in a way that allows for efficient retrieval, insertion, updating, and deletion of information. Common database management systems (DBMS) include SQL-based systems like **MySQL, SQL Server, SQLite**, and **PostgreSQL**.

   Basic Database Concepts:

   o **Tables**: Data in a database is organized into tables, which consist of rows and columns.

   o **SQL (Structured Query Language)**: A language used to query, insert, update, and delete data in a relational database.

   o **CRUD Operations**: The basic operations for interacting with a database: **Create, Read, Update, Delete**.

2. **Using ADO.NET to Connect to a Database ADO.NET** is a data access technology in C# that provides the means to

connect to and manipulate data in a database. ADO.NET supports a variety of databases and is based on the **.NET Framework.**

Core ADO.NET Components:

o **Connection**: Represents the connection to the database (e.g., SqlConnection for SQL Server).

o **Command**: Represents an SQL statement or stored procedure that is executed against the database (e.g., SqlCommand).

o **DataReader**: Provides a way to read data from the database in a forward-only manner.

o **DataAdapter**: Acts as a bridge to populate a DataSet or DataTable with data from the database.

Establishing a Database Connection: You need a connection string to establish a connection to a database. The connection string contains details like the database server, database name, and authentication credentials.

Example Connection String (for SQL Server):

csharp

```
string                connectionString                =
"Server=myServerAddress;Database=myDataBase;User
Id=myUsername;Password=myPassword;";
```

Example of Connecting to SQL Server using ADO.NET:

csharp

```csharp
using System.Data.SqlClient;

string connectionString = "your_connection_string_here";
SqlConnection connection = new SqlConnection(connectionString);
connection.Open();
```

3. **Performing CRUD Operations with ADO.NET**
   - o **Create**: Insert data into the database.
   - o **Read**: Retrieve data from the database.
   - o **Update**: Modify existing data in the database.
   - o **Delete**: Remove data from the database.

Example of Executing a Command (Inserting Data):

csharp

```csharp
SqlCommand command = new SqlCommand("INSERT INTO Users
(Name, Email) VALUES (@Name, @Email)", connection);
command.Parameters.AddWithValue("@Name", "John Doe");
command.Parameters.AddWithValue("@Email",
"john.doe@example.com");
command.ExecuteNonQuery();
```

4. **Handling Errors** When working with databases, errors can occur (e.g., connection issues, SQL errors). It's essential to

handle exceptions properly using try-catch blocks to prevent application crashes.

Real-World Example: A Basic Application That Stores User Data in an SQL Database

In this example, we will create a simple application that connects to an SQL database to store user information (name and email). The application will perform the following operations:

1. Connect to the database.
2. Insert user data (name and email) into a Users table.
3. Retrieve and display the stored data.

Steps:

1. Set up an SQL database with a table Users to store user information.
2. Use ADO.NET to insert new user data into the database.
3. Retrieve and display the stored data.

SQL Database Setup:

First, you need to create a database and a Users table. Here's an example SQL script to create the table:

sql

```sql
CREATE DATABASE UserData;

USE UserData;

CREATE TABLE Users (
    Id INT PRIMARY KEY IDENTITY(1,1),
    Name NVARCHAR(100),
    Email NVARCHAR(100)
);
```

C# Application Code:

csharp

```csharp
using System;
using System.Data.SqlClient;

class Program
{
    static string connectionString = "Server=myServerAddress;Database=UserData;User Id=myUsername;Password=myPassword;";

    static void Main(string[] args)
    {
        // Insert user data into the database
        InsertUserData("John Doe", "john.doe@example.com");

        // Retrieve and display user data
        DisplayUsers();
    }
```

```csharp
// Method to insert user data into the Users table
static void InsertUserData(string name, string email)
{
    using (SqlConnection connection = new SqlConnection(connectionString))
    {
        try
        {
            connection.Open();
            string query = "INSERT INTO Users (Name, Email) VALUES (@Name, @Email)";
            SqlCommand command = new SqlCommand(query, connection);
            command.Parameters.AddWithValue("@Name", name);
            command.Parameters.AddWithValue("@Email", email);

            command.ExecuteNonQuery();  // Execute the insert command
            Console.WriteLine("User data inserted successfully.");
        }
        catch (Exception ex)
        {
            Console.WriteLine("Error: " + ex.Message);
        }
    }
}

// Method to display all users from the Users table
static void DisplayUsers()
{
    using (SqlConnection connection = new SqlConnection(connectionString))
    {
```

```
try
{
    connection.Open();
    string query = "SELECT * FROM Users";
    SqlCommand command = new SqlCommand(query, connection);
    SqlDataReader reader = command.ExecuteReader();

    Console.WriteLine("Users in the database:");
    while (reader.Read())
    {
        Console.WriteLine($"ID: {reader["Id"]}, Name: {reader["Name"]},
Email: {reader["Email"]}");
    }
}
catch (Exception ex)
{
    Console.WriteLine("Error: " + ex.Message);
}
    }
  }
}
```

Explanation:

1. **Connection String**: The connection string contains the database connection information, including the server address, database name, username, and password.

2. **InsertUserData Method**: This method establishes a connection to the database and executes an INSERT query to add a new user to the Users table. The method uses

SqlCommand and parameterized queries (@Name and @Email) to insert the user data securely.

3. **DisplayUsers Method**: This method retrieves all user records from the Users table using a SELECT query. It then displays the retrieved data in the console.

4. **Error Handling**: Both methods use try-catch blocks to handle any errors that may occur while interacting with the database, such as connection issues or SQL errors.

Output Example:

yaml

User data inserted successfully.
Users in the database:
ID: 1, Name: John Doe, Email: john.doe@example.com

Real-World Use Case

This application can be used in a variety of real-world scenarios, such as:

- **User Registration Systems**: Storing user details (e.g., name, email, and password) for a web or desktop application.
- **CRM (Customer Relationship Management) Systems**: Storing customer information, including name, contact details, and order history.

- **Inventory Management Systems**: Storing product details, such as name, price, quantity, and SKU in a database.

By understanding how to interact with databases using ADO.NET, you can create applications that store, retrieve, and manage large sets of data, ensuring that your application has a persistent data layer.

Chapter 20: Introduction to Multithreading

Topics:

1. **What is Multithreading?** Multithreading is a programming technique that allows multiple threads to run concurrently, enabling your program to perform multiple tasks at the same time. Each thread is a lightweight sub-process that can run independently and perform its own task while the main thread or other threads continue their execution.

   Key Concepts:

   - **Thread**: A thread is the smallest unit of execution in a program. Each thread has its own execution path.
   - **Main Thread**: The main thread is the entry point of your application. It's the first thread that gets created when the program starts.
   - **Concurrency vs. Parallelism**:
     - **Concurrency**: Multiple tasks are in progress, but not necessarily simultaneously (tasks may take turns running).
     - **Parallelism**: Tasks are literally running at the same time on multiple cores or processors.

2. **Why Use Multithreading?**

- o **Improved Performance**: By running multiple tasks concurrently, you can improve the responsiveness and performance of your application, especially when performing I/O-bound operations (e.g., downloading files, reading/writing to files, etc.).

- o **Better Resource Utilization**: Multithreading allows for efficient utilization of multi-core processors.

- o **Responsive Applications**: Multithreading is essential for building responsive applications that perform tasks like background processing without freezing the user interface (UI).

3. **Creating and Managing Threads in C#** In C#, threads are created using the Thread class from the System.Threading namespace. You can start a new thread by creating an instance of the Thread class and passing a method to execute.

- o **Creating and Starting a Thread**:

csharp

```csharp
using System;
using System.Threading;

class Program
{
    static void Main(string[] args)
    {
```

```
        Thread thread = new Thread(MyMethod); // Create a new
thread
        thread.Start();  // Start the thread
    }

    static void MyMethod()
    {
        Console.WriteLine("Running on a separate thread!");
    }
}
```

- o **Thread Synchronization**: In cases where multiple threads are accessing shared data, synchronization mechanisms like **locks** (lock keyword) can be used to avoid conflicts and ensure thread safety.

4. **Thread Pooling** C# provides a **ThreadPool**, which is a collection of threads that can be used to perform background work. Instead of creating a new thread for each task, you can queue tasks in the thread pool, which optimizes thread management and reduces the overhead of creating and destroying threads.

Using ThreadPool:

csharp

```
ThreadPool.QueueUserWorkItem(MyMethod);
```

5. **Managing Threads and Task Parallel Library (TPL)** In addition to Thread and ThreadPool, the **Task Parallel Library (TPL)** provides a higher-level API for managing concurrency in C#. The Task class abstracts thread management and provides better support for parallelism, cancellation, and exception handling.

Real-World Example: A Program That Performs Tasks Concurrently (e.g., Downloading Files)

In this example, we will create a simple program that simulates downloading files concurrently using multithreading. The program will simulate downloading by performing a time-consuming task (e.g., waiting for a few seconds) on multiple threads at the same time.

Steps:

1. Use multiple threads to simulate downloading files concurrently.
2. Each thread will perform a "download" task (simulated with Thread.Sleep).
3. Display the progress of each download.

Code:

csharp

```csharp
using System;
using System.Threading;

class Program
{
    static void Main(string[] args)
    {
        // Start multiple threads to simulate downloading files concurrently
        Thread thread1 = new Thread(() => DownloadFile("File1"));
        Thread thread2 = new Thread(() => DownloadFile("File2"));
        Thread thread3 = new Thread(() => DownloadFile("File3"));

        // Start the threads
        thread1.Start();
        thread2.Start();
        thread3.Start();

        // Wait for all threads to finish
        thread1.Join();
        thread2.Join();
        thread3.Join();

        Console.WriteLine("All downloads completed!");
    }

    static void DownloadFile(string fileName)
    {
        Console.WriteLine($"Starting download of {fileName}...");
        // Simulate a time-consuming download task
```

```
Thread.Sleep(3000);  // Simulating a 3-second download
Console.WriteLine($"{fileName} downloaded!");
    }
}
```

Explanation:

1. **Threads for Concurrent Download**: The DownloadFile method simulates a file download by using Thread.Sleep(3000), which pauses the thread for 3 seconds to simulate the download time. This method is executed by multiple threads, allowing the files to be "downloaded" concurrently.

2. **Thread.Start()**: This method is used to start the threads, each simulating the download of a different file.

3. **Thread.Join()**: This method ensures that the main thread waits for all the download threads to finish before printing "All downloads completed!".

4. **Thread.Sleep()**: This is used to simulate a time-consuming task (in this case, the download of files).

Output Example:

css

```
Starting download of File1...
Starting download of File2...
Starting download of File3...
File1 downloaded!
File2 downloaded!
```

File3 downloaded!

All downloads completed!

Real-World Use Case

This multithreading example can be applied in various real-world scenarios where tasks can be performed concurrently, such as:

- **Web Scraping**: Downloading multiple web pages at once, which reduces the overall time required.
- **File Processing**: Processing multiple large files concurrently (e.g., converting, compressing, or moving files).
- **Network Communication**: Handling multiple network connections concurrently, such as managing multiple downloads or uploads in a server-client application.
- **UI Applications**: Performing background tasks (e.g., data fetching or processing) in a multithreaded manner to keep the UI responsive and prevent it from freezing.

By understanding and utilizing multithreading, you can significantly improve the performance and responsiveness of your applications, making them more efficient in handling time-consuming tasks.

Chapter 21: Creating Custom Controls

Topics:

1. **What are Custom Controls?** Custom controls are user-defined controls that extend the functionality of standard controls or create entirely new controls with specific behavior and appearance. In Windows Forms, custom controls are often needed when built-in controls do not fulfill the requirements of the application, such as for unique visual styles or specialized functionality.

   Key Benefits of Custom Controls:

   o **Reusability**: Once created, custom controls can be reused across multiple forms or applications.

   o **Encapsulation**: Custom controls encapsulate specific behavior and visual elements, simplifying code maintenance.

   o **Extensibility**: Custom controls can extend existing controls to include additional functionality or handle specific events.

2. **Designing Custom Controls in Windows Forms** Custom controls can be created by either:

   o **Deriving from an existing control**: This is the most common method and involves inheriting from a base control like Button, TextBox, or ProgressBar and overriding its methods to change its behavior.

- o **Deriving from Control**: This allows you to create an entirely new control from scratch. You will need to handle painting, event handling, and layout.

3. **Steps to Create a Custom Control**:

   - o **Step 1: Derive from a Control Class**: You can either inherit from a base control like Button or Panel, or derive directly from the Control class to build your custom control from the ground up.

   - o **Step 2: Override Painting Methods**: You will need to override the OnPaint method to define the custom appearance of your control.

   - o **Step 3: Handle User Interactions**: Implement event handlers (like Click, MouseMove, etc.) to make the control interactive.

   - o **Step 4: Add Custom Properties and Methods**: Customize the control with properties that can be set by the user (e.g., setting a progress percentage in a custom progress bar).

4. **Handling Custom Painting with OnPaint** Custom painting is done by overriding the OnPaint method. This is where you can define how the control is rendered, including background colors, borders, text, or other elements.

Example of overriding OnPaint:

csharp

```csharp
protected override void OnPaint(PaintEventArgs e)
{
    base.OnPaint(e);
    Graphics g = e.Graphics;
    // Custom drawing code here
}
```

5. **Handling Layout and Resizing** When creating custom controls, you may want to control how the control is sized and laid out. You can override the OnResize method to adjust the layout when the control is resized.

Real-World Example: A Custom Progress Bar Control

In this example, we will create a custom progress bar control that displays the progress of a task. The control will allow you to:

- Set the progress percentage.
- Customize the appearance, such as the color of the progress bar.

Steps:

1. Create a custom control class that inherits from Control.
2. Override the OnPaint method to render the progress bar.

3. Add properties like Progress to control the progress value.

Code:

csharp

```csharp
using System;
using System.Drawing;
using System.Windows.Forms;

public class CustomProgressBar : Control
{
    private int progress = 0;  // Progress value between 0 and 100

    public int Progress
    {
        get { return progress; }
        set
        {
            // Ensure the progress is between 0 and 100
            if (value < 0)
                progress = 0;
            else if (value > 100)
                progress = 100;
            else
                progress = value;

            // Redraw the control when the progress changes
            Invalidate();
        }
    }
}
```

```csharp
public CustomProgressBar()
{
    // Set the size of the control (default size)
    this.Width = 200;
    this.Height = 30;
}


// Override the OnPaint method to customize the drawing of the control
protected override void OnPaint(PaintEventArgs e)
{
    base.OnPaint(e);
    Graphics g = e.Graphics;

    // Define the background and progress bar colors
    Color backgroundColor = Color.Gray;
    Color progressBarColor = Color.Green;

    // Draw the background of the progress bar
    g.FillRectangle(new SolidBrush(backgroundColor), 0, 0, this.Width, this.Height);

    // Draw the progress bar based on the current progress value
    int progressWidth = (int)((progress / 100.0) * this.Width);
    g.FillRectangle(new SolidBrush(progressBarColor), 0, 0, progressWidth, this.Height);

    // Optionally, draw text in the middle of the progress bar
    string progressText = $"{progress}%";
    Font font = new Font("Arial", 10);
```

```csharp
    SizeF textSize = g.MeasureString(progressText, font);
    g.DrawString(progressText,    font,    Brushes.White,    (this.Width    -
textSize.Width) / 2, (this.Height - textSize.Height) / 2);
  }
}


public class MainForm : Form
{
  private CustomProgressBar progressBar;
  private Timer timer;
  private int currentProgress = 0;

  public MainForm()
  {
    this.Text = "Custom Progress Bar Example";
    this.Size = new Size(300, 150);

    // Create and add the custom progress bar control
    progressBar = new CustomProgressBar();
    progressBar.Location = new Point(50, 50);
    this.Controls.Add(progressBar);

    // Set up a timer to simulate progress
    timer = new Timer();
    timer.Interval = 100;  // Update progress every 100ms
    timer.Tick += Timer_Tick;
    timer.Start();
  }

  private void Timer_Tick(object sender, EventArgs e)
```

```
{
    // Simulate task progress
    if (currentProgress < 100)
    {
        currentProgress++;
        progressBar.Progress = currentProgress;
    }
    else
    {
        timer.Stop();  // Stop the timer when the progress reaches 100%
        MessageBox.Show("Task Complete!");
    }
}

static void Main()
{
    Application.Run(new MainForm());
}
}
```

Explanation:

1. **CustomProgressBar Class**:
    - **Progress Property**: This property holds the progress value between 0 and 100. When the progress is set, the control is invalidated (redrawn) to reflect the new progress.
    - **OnPaint Method**: This method is overridden to handle custom rendering. It draws the background of

the progress bar and then fills a portion of it based on the current progress. The text displaying the percentage is also drawn in the center.

2. **MainForm Class**:

   o   A CustomProgressBar is created and added to the form.

   o   A Timer is used to simulate a task, updating the progress every 100 milliseconds. The progress bar's value is updated, and once the progress reaches 100%, the timer stops, and a message is shown to indicate that the task is complete.

Output Example:

The application will show a window with a custom progress bar. The progress bar will fill up over time, simulating a task, and will display the progress percentage in the center.

Real-World Use Case

Creating custom controls can be extremely useful in real-world applications, such as:

- **Custom Progress Bars**: As seen in this example, progress bars that are more visually appealing or have custom behavior (like showing an estimated time remaining).

- **Custom Input Controls**: Building custom input fields, such as a date picker or a masked input control for phone numbers or credit card numbers.
- **UI Enhancements**: Adding specialized visual elements to enhance the user experience, such as custom buttons, sliders, or interactive charts.

By creating custom controls in Windows Forms, you can improve the usability and appearance of your application, providing a tailored experience for your users.

Chapter 22: Using External Libraries and APIs

Topics:

1. **What Are External Libraries and APIs?**
   o **External Libraries**: These are pre-written pieces of code that you can use in your application to avoid reinventing the wheel. External libraries can provide functionality for tasks like data manipulation, UI controls, or database access. In .NET, libraries are typically packaged as **NuGet packages**.

   o **APIs (Application Programming Interfaces)**: An API is a set of rules and protocols that allow one software application to interact with another. APIs can provide access to remote services, like retrieving data from a web service or interacting with external systems (e.g., social media, weather data, payment systems, etc.).

   Examples:

   o **External Libraries**: Newtonsoft.Json (for working with JSON), EntityFramework (for database access), NLog (for logging).

  o **APIs**: Weather APIs, Payment APIs (Stripe, PayPal),
     Social Media APIs (Twitter, Facebook).

2. **Integrating Third-Party Libraries in .NET** .NET provides
   a tool called **NuGet** for managing external libraries and
   packages. You can use NuGet to search for, install, and
   update libraries in your project. NuGet makes it easy to
   integrate third-party functionality into your application.

   Steps to Install a NuGet Package:

   o Open **Visual Studio**.
   o Go to **Tools > NuGet Package Manager > Manage
      NuGet Packages for Solution**.
   o Search for the desired library (e.g., Newtonsoft.Json).
   o Click **Install** to add the library to your project.

3. **Using External APIs** To interact with an external API, you
   typically need to:

   o Send an HTTP request (usually a GET request) to the
      API endpoint.
   o Receive the data in a specified format (e.g., JSON or
      XML).
   o Parse and process the data to display it in your
      application.

In .NET, the **HttpClient** class from the System.Net.Http namespace is commonly used for sending HTTP requests and receiving responses.

Steps to Use an API:

- o **Send an HTTP Request**: Use HttpClient to send a request to the API.
- o **Parse the Response**: Typically, the response is in JSON or XML format. You can parse the data using libraries like Newtonsoft.Json for JSON.
- o **Display the Data**: Once parsed, the data can be displayed in your application.

4. **Authentication for APIs** Some APIs require authentication via API keys, OAuth tokens, or other methods. You usually pass these credentials as part of the HTTP request headers.

Example of setting an API key in the request headers:

csharp

```
HttpClient client = new HttpClient();
client.DefaultRequestHeaders.Add("Authorization",        "Bearer
your_api_key_here");
```

Real-World Example: A Program That Fetches Data from a Public API (e.g., Weather Data)

In this example, we will create a C# program that fetches weather data from a public API (e.g., the **OpenWeatherMap API**). The program will:

- Send an HTTP request to the API.
- Parse the JSON response.
- Display the weather data (e.g., temperature and conditions) to the user.

Steps:

1. Create an account at OpenWeatherMap and get an API key.
2. Install the Newtonsoft.Json NuGet package to parse JSON data.
3. Write code to fetch the weather data and display it.

Install NuGet Package:

- Open the **NuGet Package Manager** in Visual Studio.
- Search for Newtonsoft.Json and install it.

Code:

csharp

```csharp
using System;
using System.Net.Http;
using System.Threading.Tasks;
using Newtonsoft.Json;
```

```csharp
public class WeatherResponse
{
    public Main Main { get; set; }
    public Weather[] Weather { get; set; }

    public class Main
    {
        public float Temp { get; set; }
        public int Humidity { get; set; }
    }

    public class Weather
    {
        public string Description { get; set; }
    }
}

class Program
{
    static async Task Main(string[] args)
    {
        string apiKey = "your_api_key_here"; // Replace with your API key
        string city = "London"; // Example city
        string apiUrl = $"http://api.openweathermap.org/data/2.5/weather?q={city}&appid={apiKey}&units=metric";

        HttpClient client = new HttpClient();

        try
```

```
        {
            // Sending the GET request
            HttpResponseMessage response = await client.GetAsync(apiUrl);
            response.EnsureSuccessStatusCode();   // Throws an exception if the
response is not successful

            // Reading and parsing the JSON response
            string responseData = await response.Content.ReadAsStringAsync();
            WeatherResponse                weatherData                =
JsonConvert.DeserializeObject<WeatherResponse>(responseData);

            // Displaying the weather data
            Console.WriteLine($"Weather in {city}:");
            Console.WriteLine($"Temperature: {weatherData.Main.Temp}°C");
            Console.WriteLine($"Humidity: {weatherData.Main.Humidity}%");
            Console.WriteLine($"Condition:
{weatherData.Weather[0].Description}");
        }
        catch (Exception ex)
        {
            Console.WriteLine($"Error fetching data: {ex.Message}");
        }
    }
}
```

Explanation:

1. **WeatherResponse Class**:
   - o   This class models the structure of the data returned by the OpenWeatherMap API. The Main class holds

the temperature and humidity, and the Weather class contains the weather description (e.g., "clear sky").

2. **HttpClient**:

   o An instance of HttpClient is created to send a GET request to the OpenWeatherMap API, using the provided city and apiKey.

3. **Deserializing JSON Data**:

   o The response from the API is in JSON format. The JsonConvert.DeserializeObject method from the Newtonsoft.Json library is used to convert the JSON string into an object of type WeatherResponse.

4. **Handling Errors**:

   o The try-catch block is used to handle any errors, such as network issues or invalid API keys.

5. **Displaying the Data**:

   o The program then prints the weather information (temperature, humidity, and description) to the console.

Output Example:

yaml

Weather in London:
Temperature: 15°C
Humidity: 82%
Condition: broken clouds

Real-World Use Case

This example of integrating an external API (OpenWeatherMap) can be expanded and applied in various real-world scenarios, such as:

- **Weather Applications**: Displaying current weather information based on user input or geolocation.
- **Social Media Integrations**: Fetching posts, tweets, or other content from external social media APIs (e.g., Twitter, Facebook).
- **Financial Applications**: Fetching stock prices, exchange rates, or financial data from external APIs (e.g., Alpha Vantage, Yahoo Finance).
- **E-Commerce Applications**: Integrating payment gateways, product catalogs, or inventory systems via APIs (e.g., PayPal, Stripe, Shopify API).

By understanding how to use external libraries and APIs, you can extend the functionality of your applications and provide rich, dynamic features that rely on external data sources or services.

Chapter 23: Building and Deploying a Windows Application

Topics:

1. **Packaging and Deploying Your Application as an Executable** Packaging and deploying an application means preparing it for distribution and installation on other computers. In C#, Windows Forms applications are typically compiled into **.exe** files, which can be run directly on Windows operating systems.

    o **Building an Executable**: When you build a Windows Forms application in Visual Studio, it compiles your code into an executable (.exe) file located in the **bin** folder of your project directory.

    o **Release Configuration**: You need to build your application in **Release** mode rather than **Debug** mode for the final version that you will distribute.

    ▪ Go to **Build > Configuration Manager** in Visual Studio and ensure the build configuration is set to **Release**.

    o **Generating the Executable**: After building the project, the output .exe file will be located in the project's **bin\Release** directory. This file can be run directly or packaged into an installer.

2. **Creating an Installer** While distributing the .exe directly is possible, it's more common to create an **installer** that handles the installation process, including copying files to appropriate directories, adding registry entries, and creating shortcuts.

An installer typically performs the following tasks:

- o Installs the application files (e.g., .exe, .dll files, etc.) to the target machine.
- o Registers the application in the **Start Menu**.
- o Creates shortcuts on the desktop or Start Menu.
- o Configures system requirements like .NET Framework or other dependencies.
- o Handles uninstallation of the application.

Common Tools for Creating Installers:

- o **Inno Setup**: A free script-driven installation system for creating Windows installers.
- o **WiX Toolset**: A powerful toolset that uses XML-based scripting to create MSI installers.
- o **Visual Studio Installer Projects**: An easy-to-use method for creating basic installers directly in Visual Studio.

3. **Using Visual Studio Installer Projects** Visual Studio provides a project type called **Installer Project** that can be used to create an installer for your application.

Steps to Create an Installer with Visual Studio:

- o **Step 1**: Install the "Microsoft Visual Studio Installer Projects" extension if it's not already available in your version of Visual Studio.
  - Go to **Extensions > Manage Extensions** in Visual Studio and search for "Installer Projects".
- o **Step 2**: Create a new **Setup Project**:
  - Go to **File > New > Project**.
  - Search for "Setup Project" and create a new one.
- o **Step 3**: Add your application's files (like .exe, .dll, etc.) to the setup project by right-clicking on the **Application Folder** in the **File System** view.
- o **Step 4**: Configure your installation settings, such as adding desktop shortcuts or Start Menu entries.
- o **Step 5**: Build the setup project, which will generate an installer (.msi file) that you can distribute.

4. **Handling Dependencies** If your application depends on external libraries or specific versions of the .NET

Framework, you may need to include those dependencies in the installer or ensure they are installed on the target machine.

- o **.NET Framework**: If your application targets a specific version of .NET Framework, you can configure the installer to check for and install the required version if it's not already present.
- o **Third-Party Libraries**: If your app uses third-party libraries (e.g., Newtonsoft.Json), include those .dll files in the installer package.

Real-World Example: Building a Simple Installer for Your Windows Forms App

In this example, we will walk through the process of building a simple installer for a basic Windows Forms application using Visual Studio's Installer Project. The application will be a simple Windows Forms app that displays a message when a button is clicked.

Steps:

1. **Create the Windows Forms Application**: First, let's create a simple Windows Forms application in Visual Studio.
   - o Open Visual Studio and create a new **Windows Forms App (.NET Framework)** project.
   - o Add a button and a label to the form.

o Add a simple event handler for the button to display a message on the label.

Code for the Windows Forms Application:

csharp

```
using System;
using System.Windows.Forms;

namespace SimpleApp
{
    public partial class MainForm : Form
    {
        public MainForm()
        {
            InitializeComponent();
        }

        private void button1_Click(object sender, EventArgs e)
        {
            label1.Text = "Hello, world!";
        }
    }
}
```

2. **Install the Installer Project Extension**: If you haven't already, install the **Installer Project** extension:

o Go to **Extensions > Manage Extensions** in Visual Studio.

- o   Search for **Installer Projects** and install it.

3. **Create a Setup Project**:

   - o   Go to **File > New > Project**.

   - o   Search for **Setup Project** in the project templates and create a new one.

4. **Add Your Application Files**:

   - o   In the **Solution Explorer**, right-click on your Setup Project and choose **View > File System**.

   - o   Under the **Application Folder**, right-click and select **Add > Project Output**.

   - o   Choose your **Primary Output** (the compiled .exe file) from the Windows Forms app.

5. **Configure the Installer**:

   - o   Right-click on the **File System** in the setup project, and select **Add Special Folder > Desktop** to add a shortcut to the desktop.

   - o   Right-click on the **Desktop** folder, choose **Create New Shortcut**, and select your application's .exe file.

6. **Build the Installer**:

   - o   After adding the necessary files and configuring the setup, right-click on the setup project and select **Build**.

   - o   This will generate a .msi file in the output folder.

7. **Test the Installer**:

- o After the build is completed, locate the .msi file in your project directory.
- o Run the .msi file to install the application.
- o Once installed, the application should be available in the Start Menu or on the desktop (if you created a shortcut), and running it should show the Windows Forms application.

Real-World Use Case

This example of building and deploying a Windows Forms application using an installer can be applied to many real-world scenarios:

- **Business Software**: Packaging enterprise applications that need to be deployed across multiple machines.
- **Utilities**: Creating standalone applications that can be easily installed and uninstalled.
- **Updates and Patches**: Packaging updates to existing software or creating automatic patching systems.

By mastering the process of building and deploying Windows applications, you ensure that your applications can be easily distributed to users, installed with ease, and uninstalled when necessary. Creating an installer provides a smooth installation experience and allows for better control over the installation process.

Chapter 24: Best Practices for C# Programming

Topics:

1. **Writing Clean, Maintainable Code** Writing clean, maintainable code is essential for creating applications that are easy to understand, extend, and maintain over time. Clean code makes collaboration smoother and reduces the likelihood of introducing bugs. It involves following principles such as simplicity, readability, and consistency.

   Key Principles of Clean Code:

   o **Meaningful Names**: Use descriptive and meaningful names for variables, methods, and classes. This helps other developers (or your future self) to understand the purpose of the code.

   o **Avoiding Duplication**: DRY (Don't Repeat Yourself) principle encourages you to eliminate code duplication by abstracting common functionality into methods or classes.

   o **Small Functions**: Break down complex tasks into smaller, single-purpose methods. This makes your code easier to read and test.

- o **Commenting**: While you should aim to write self-explanatory code, comments can be used for complex logic or to explain the "why" behind certain decisions. Avoid redundant comments that explain the obvious.
- o **Consistent Formatting**: Use consistent indentation, spacing, and line breaks to make your code more readable.

2. **Understanding Common C# Conventions** C# has specific naming and formatting conventions that help make code more readable and consistent across projects.

Common C# Naming Conventions:

- o **PascalCase**: Used for class names, method names, and property names (e.g., MyClass, GetUserData).
- o **camelCase**: Used for local variables and parameters (e.g., userData, customerName).
- o **UPPERCASE**: Used for constant values and static readonly fields (e.g., MAX_VALUE, DEFAULT_TIMEOUT).
- o **Prefixing Interfaces**: Interfaces are often prefixed with an "I" (e.g., IEnumerable, IDisposable).
- o **Verb-Noun Method Names**: Method names should typically be in verb-noun format to reflect the action (e.g., CalculateTotal, SaveFile).

Code Formatting:

- o Use **spaces** around operators (=, +, -, etc.) and after commas (e.g., int sum = a + b;).
- o Indentation should be consistent (usually **4 spaces** per level).
- o Place **curly braces** on the same line for methods and control statements (e.g., if (condition) {).

3. **Refactoring Code for Maintainability** Refactoring is the process of restructuring existing code to improve its design, readability, and maintainability without changing its external behavior. Refactoring helps in improving code quality and making future modifications easier.

Common Refactoring Techniques:

- o **Extract Method**: If a method is too long or performs multiple tasks, break it down into smaller, more focused methods.
- o **Rename Variables and Methods**: Ensure that names are meaningful and describe the data or functionality accurately.
- o **Remove Code Duplication**: Consolidate repeated logic into a single method or class to avoid redundancy.

- o **Simplify Conditional Logic**: If you have complex nested if-else statements, consider using early returns or extracting conditions into well-named methods.

4. **Writing Unit Tests** Unit tests are an essential part of writing maintainable code. They ensure that individual pieces of functionality work as expected. Writing tests helps catch bugs early and provides a safety net for refactoring.

Unit Testing Principles:

- o **Test One Thing**: Each unit test should focus on a single unit of functionality.
- o **Arrange-Act-Assert (AAA)**: This pattern helps structure your unit tests:
  - **Arrange**: Set up the test scenario.
  - **Act**: Perform the action or method call.
  - **Assert**: Verify the result.
- o **Mocking**: Use mocking frameworks (e.g., Moq) to isolate dependencies when testing.

Real-World Example: Refactoring an Existing Application to Follow Best Practices

In this example, we will refactor an existing C# Windows Forms application that calculates the total price of items in a shopping cart.

The original code lacks clean structure and is hard to maintain. We will improve the code by applying clean code principles and best practices.

Original Code (Before Refactoring):

csharp

```csharp
public class ShoppingCart
{
    public List<Item> Items { get; set; }

    public ShoppingCart()
    {
        Items = new List<Item>();
    }

    public double CalculateTotal()
    {
        double total = 0;
        foreach (var item in Items)
        {
            total = total + item.Price * item.Quantity;
        }
        return total;
    }

    public void DisplayCartSummary()
    {
        Console.WriteLine("Shopping Cart Summary");
        foreach (var item in Items)
```

```
    {
        Console.WriteLine("Item: " + item.Name + ", Price: " + item.Price + ",
Quantity: " + item.Quantity);
    }
    Console.WriteLine("Total: " + CalculateTotal());
  }
}

public class Item
{
    public string Name { get; set; }
    public double Price { get; set; }
    public int Quantity { get; set; }
}
```

Issues:

- **Lack of meaningful variable names**: The method CalculateTotal has a variable total, which could be more descriptive.
- **Hard to maintain**: The DisplayCartSummary method does two things: displaying the summary and calculating the total, which violates the **Single Responsibility Principle**.
- **No unit tests**: The current code is not easily testable.

Refactored Code (After Refactoring):

csharp

```
public class ShoppingCart
```

```csharp
{
    private readonly List<Item> items;

    public ShoppingCart()
    {
        items = new List<Item>();
    }

    public void AddItem(Item item)
    {
        if (item != null)
        {
            items.Add(item);
        }
    }

    public double GetTotalPrice()
    {
        return items.Sum(item => item.CalculateTotalPrice());
    }

    public void DisplayCartSummary()
    {
        Console.WriteLine("Shopping Cart Summary");
        foreach (var item in items)
        {
            item.DisplayItem();
        }
        Console.WriteLine($"Total Price: {GetTotalPrice():C}");
    }
```

```
}

public class Item
{
    public string Name { get; set; }
    public double Price { get; set; }
    public int Quantity { get; set; }

    public double CalculateTotalPrice()
    {
        return Price * Quantity;
    }

    public void DisplayItem()
    {
        Console.WriteLine($"Item:   {Name},   Price:   {Price:C},   Quantity:
{Quantity}");
    }
}
```

Refactor Explanation:

1. **Meaningful Names**:
   - Renamed the method CalculateTotal to GetTotalPrice for clarity.
   - Renamed the loop variable item in the ShoppingCart class to items for consistency.

2. **Separation of Concerns**:

- o Moved the logic for calculating the total price and displaying item details into their respective methods in the Item class, improving modularity and single responsibility.

3. **Method Extraction**:
   - o Extracted the method CalculateTotalPrice() from the Item class, making it easier to manage and test.

4. **Improved Code Readability**:
   - o The DisplayCartSummary method now only handles displaying the cart summary, and the total calculation is delegated to the ShoppingCart class via the GetTotalPrice method.

5. **Unit Testing**:
   - o Now, we can unit test Item.CalculateTotalPrice() independently from ShoppingCart, and the ShoppingCart.GetTotalPrice() can also be tested separately.

Unit Test Example:

```csharp
using Xunit;

public class ShoppingCartTests
{
    [Fact]
    public void CalculateTotalPrice_ShouldReturnCorrectTotal()
```

```
{
    var item1 = new Item { Name = "Apple", Price = 1.00, Quantity = 3 };
    var item2 = new Item { Name = "Banana", Price = 0.50, Quantity = 2 };

    var cart = new ShoppingCart();
    cart.AddItem(item1);
    cart.AddItem(item2);

    double totalPrice = cart.GetTotalPrice();

    Assert.Equal(4.00, totalPrice);  // 3 * 1.00 + 2 * 0.50 = 4.00
}
}
```

Real-World Use Case

These best practices are applicable in many real-world scenarios, including:

- **Large-Scale Applications**: In business software, following best practices makes your codebase more maintainable and scalable as the application grows.
- **Collaborative Development**: Writing clean, maintainable code ensures that multiple developers can work on the project without causing conflicts or bugs.

- **Customer-Facing Applications**: In applications that customers interact with, following best practices results in a more stable, user-friendly, and bug-free experience.

By following these clean coding principles and applying refactoring techniques, you can ensure that your C# applications are maintainable, scalable, and easy to understand for both yourself and your team.

Chapter 25: Conclusion and Next Steps

Topics:

1. **Summarizing Key Learnings** Over the course of this journey, we have covered a wide range of topics that will help you become proficient in C# programming and Windows Forms development. Here's a quick recap of the key concepts we've explored:

    o **Basic C# Syntax**: You learned the fundamental building blocks of C#, including variables, data types, operators, control flow (if-else, loops), and methods.

    o **Object-Oriented Programming (OOP)**: We explored key OOP concepts like classes, objects, inheritance, polymorphism, and encapsulation. These principles help in creating structured, reusable, and maintainable code.

    o **Windows Forms Development**: You became familiar with creating user interfaces using Windows Forms, designing controls, handling events, and making your applications interactive.

    o **Data Management**: We delved into working with databases using ADO.NET, retrieving, storing, and manipulating data.

    o **Multithreading**: You learned how to execute tasks concurrently, improving the responsiveness of applications by performing background operations without freezing the UI.

o **External Libraries and APIs**: We discussed how to integrate third-party libraries and consume external APIs (e.g., fetching weather data from OpenWeatherMap) to extend the functionality of your applications.

o **Best Practices**: You learned the importance of clean, maintainable code, adhering to C# conventions, and applying refactoring techniques to improve code quality.

2. **Resources for Further Study** To continue growing as a C# developer, it's important to keep learning and practicing. Below are some resources and recommendations for further study:

   o **Official Documentation**:
      - Microsoft C# Documentation
      - Windows Forms Documentation
      - ADO.NET Documentation

   o **Books**:
      - *C# 9.0 in a Nutshell* by Joseph Albahari and Ben Albahari – A comprehensive guide to C# and the .NET framework.

- ***Pro C# 8.0 and the .NET Framework*** by Andrew Troelsen – An in-depth book covering advanced topics in C# programming.

o **Online Courses and Tutorials**:
  - Microsoft Learn
  - Pluralsight
  - Udemy

o **Community and Forums**:
  - Stack Overflow – Ask questions and participate in discussions.
  - Reddit - C# – Join the C# programming community on Reddit.
  - GitHub – Explore open-source projects, contribute to repositories, and learn from other developers.

3. **Next Steps in Your Programming Journey**

As you continue your journey, there are several areas where you can focus to deepen your knowledge and become a well-rounded developer:

o **Practice and Build Projects**: Hands-on experience is the best way to solidify your skills. Start building your own applications and try to incorporate new concepts as you learn them.

o **Learn Advanced C# Topics**: Explore advanced features of C#, such as LINQ, asynchronous programming (async/await), reflection, and dependency injection. Understanding these concepts will give you a broader understanding of C# and its capabilities.

o **Get Comfortable with .NET Core/5+**: .NET Core is cross-platform and is the future of the .NET ecosystem. Transitioning from .NET Framework to .NET Core/5+ will prepare you for modern application development.

o **Explore Other Libraries and Frameworks**: In addition to Windows Forms, explore other UI frameworks like **WPF** (Windows Presentation Foundation) or **Blazor** for web development with C#. Consider learning about popular libraries like **Entity Framework** (ORM) or **Xamarin** for mobile app development.

o **Version Control**: Learn how to use Git and GitHub for version control, which is essential for managing code changes and collaborating with other developers.

o **Contribute to Open Source**: Participating in open-source projects is a great way to gain experience, collaborate with other developers, and build your portfolio.

4. **Ideas for Projects to Continue Practicing Your C# Skills**
   Building real-world projects is an excellent way to continue practicing and improving your C# skills. Below are some project ideas that can help you explore different aspects of C# programming:

   o **To-Do List Application**: Build a simple application that allows users to add, edit, delete, and mark tasks as completed. Incorporate features like file storage (for saving tasks) or a database (to store tasks persistently).

   o **Personal Finance Tracker**: Create an application that allows users to track their income, expenses, and calculate their balance. Add features like generating reports, setting budgets, and categorizing expenses.

   o **Weather App**: Use an external API (like OpenWeatherMap) to fetch and display weather data based on the user's location or a specific city.

   o **Library Management System**: Build a system to manage a library of books. Users should be able to borrow and return books, search for books, and view their borrowing history.

   o **Student Management System**: Create an application to manage student records, including adding, updating, and deleting student information. Integrate database functionality for persistent storage.

o **Multithreading File Downloader**: Build a program that uses multiple threads to download multiple files concurrently. The user should be able to see the progress of each download in real time.

o **Chat Application**: Create a simple chat application where users can communicate in real-time. Use sockets for networking, and experiment with multithreading to handle multiple clients.

Final Thoughts

Congratulations on completing this course on C# programming and Windows Forms development! By following best practices and continuing to build real-world projects, you'll continue to improve your skills and become a proficient C# developer. Remember that learning to program is a journey that never really ends — always strive to improve, explore new tools and technologies, and keep pushing the boundaries of your abilities.

Good luck, and happy coding!